MOVING ON IN SPELLING:

Strategies and Activities for the Whole Language Classroom

by Cheryl Lacey

SCHOLASTIC
PROFESSIONAL BOOKS

New York • Toronto • London • Auckland • Sydney

Acknowledgments

I would like to thank all the children, teachers, and friends who have made contributions to this book. Thanks to Terry Cooper for giving me this opportunity and for her enthusiasm. Thanks to Joan Novelli for her positive feedback and input into the publication. Thanks to my favorite little vegemites of Prep L for making teaching and learning a most rewarding experience. Thanks also to my 2LS group. What a team!

A special thank you to my father for his time, effort, and guidance.

Dedication

To my best friend for his enthusiasm,
support, and encouragement

Scholastic Inc. grants teachers permission to photocopy the reproducible pages from this book for classroom use. No other part of this publication may be reproduced in whole or in part, or stored in a retrieval system, or transmitted in any form or by any means, electronic, mechanical, photocopying, recording, or otherwise, without permission of the publisher. For information regarding permission, write to Scholastic Professional Books, 555 Broadway, New York, NY 10012-3999.

Cover design by Vincent Ceci and Frank Maiocco
Cover illustration by Vincent Ceci
Interior design by Roberto Dominguez
Interior illustrations by James Hale
Interior photographs by Cheryl Lacey
ISBN 0-590-49636-0

Table of Contents

Introduction

As many of you have discovered, a whole language approach can pave the way to teaching and learning that is real, meaningful, and fun for children. Whole language offers opportunities to create stimulating and realistic learning experiences and to provide frameworks for children to question, challenge, and seek information for themselves.

While developing my classroom program around a whole language approach, the connections between this and the integrated approach to teaching and learning became quite clear. In planning units that encouraged children to inquire, question, hypothesize, and predict, both approaches offered real reasons for children to read, research, record, discuss, and share their ideas.

Although I was satisfied with the way I integrated my curriculum, I still found spelling a concern. I addressed spelling in many class activities, such as conferencing, and modeled writing sessions, but I didn't feel I was reaching every child. In planning real and meaningful integrated units, I felt spelling had to have a purpose, too. Once again, I turned to whole language.

For children to develop an understanding and build a greater knowledge about the written word, including spelling, they need to be using it in real ways. It made sense to me then, to build a spelling program out of my writing program. I began to implement an approach to spelling that centered on children's own writings and was, therefore, entirely individualized. At the same time, I found I could follow the same basic formula for everyone.

As I planned and developed my spelling program, I constantly reminded myself of four very important factors:

- My students thoroughly enjoy participating and learning in a stimulating environment full of variety.
- My students also need routines to help them grow as independent and responsible learners.
- The individual needs of every child can be addressed within the same program.
- Time, trial and error, adaptation, and perseverance are key elements to a successful program.

The spelling strategies I use enable me to enjoy integrating language and spelling with all other curriculum areas. At the same time, I'm able to establish an individual approach to spelling that ensures that every child's needs are addressed.

I initially planned the program to suit my style and philosophy. But in sharing the strategies with colleagues, while conducting workshops and refining my own program, I've found that it blends with and supports almost any teaching style.

I trust this book will be a practical guide for you. Do as I did! Adapt, refine, elaborate, or reshape the spelling strategies within to suit your own teaching style and the needs of your students. I am sure your efforts will be rewarded.

Enjoy.

Chapter One

SPELLING IN THE INTEGRATED CURRICULUM

I f you implement an integrated curriculum in your classroom, you already know the benefits of this approach. An integrated curriculum encourages you to plan units that build links between different disciplines—language, math, science, personal development, history, geography, and so on. As you and your students make these connections, the doors to inquiry and exploration open. An integrated unit on whales, for example, might generate the following connections: How far does a whale migrating from one region to another travel? What is the history of whaling? How might whale watching adversely affect a humpback's habitat? What is a group of whales called? What are other groups of animals called? Do whales have human-like intelligence? What happens to a beached whale? How do whales use sound?

Integrated curriculums give children opportunities to be involved in creative and educational units that can be examined as one large project, rather than isolated chunks. As children absorb the concepts in an integrated curriculum, they continue to make new connections themselves. Each unit suggests new opportunities for them to explore, question, and understand their world. They can see the logic behind all that they do because they have a real purpose in mind. They seek explanations to questions, find solutions to problems, and make judgments about their results.

In looking at the way children gather and record this information, the opportunities for language development are clear. For example, a zoo excursion might inspire the following experiences, all of which involve language:

- written report about the day's outing
- class wall story
- class book
- brochure inviting others to visit the zoo
- thank-you letter to the zoo staff
- TV advertisement encouraging others to visit the zoo
- poster of a favorite animal, featuring factual information
- map highlighting main attractions
- guide book for visitors
- captions for photographs taken at the zoo
- article about the trip for the school newspaper
- presentation for another class, a school assembly, or a PTA meeting

The variety of activities shows just how diverse a unit can be. It also shows that with careful planning you can provide writing experiences that are exciting, relevant, and worthwhile. Writing is one area in particular that blends quite well with integrated units. As with the zoo activities, you can incorporate different formats, a range of presentation styles, and a variety of real purposes for presenting similar information. What's really exciting about this is that it forms an umbrella for further learning.

Each time you engage students in a writing activity, you actually create a situation where they automatically have a need to spell. An effective writing program helps equip children to meet this need.

Throughout this book, you'll see how spelling is connected to my writing program, which grows out of my integrated curriculum. By looking at the complete picture of where spelling fits into writing and into the overall curriculum, you can see how one learning outcome acts as a link to another. The flow chart on the following page, along with brief explanations of each component, can help you see these connections more clearly. Each component is discussed in greater detail throughout the book.

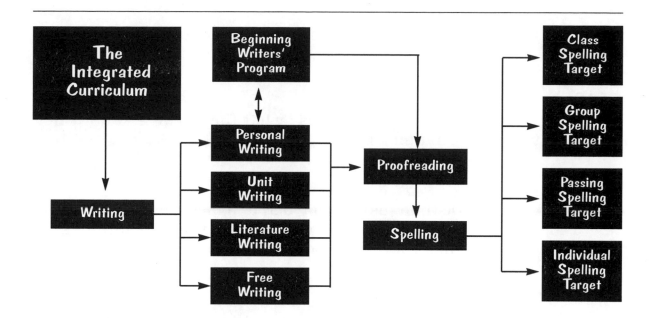

The Integrated Curriculum

The framework around which units of work are developed. It gives direction and purpose to learning.

Writing

Writing is the umbrella under which spelling belongs. Without writing, there is no place for spelling. Writing programs benefit from variety and purpose.

Beginning Writers' Program

Beginning and reluctant writers need a balanced writing program that encourages them to want to write. With a solid and positive start they can become confident and competent writers (see Chapter 4).

Personal Writing

Students can share innermost thoughts, fears, and wonders in writing. It's a marvelous way to get to know your students and for them to get to know you (see Chapter 3).

Unit Writing

Integrated units provide endless opportunities to write with variety and purpose (see Chapter 3).

Literature Writing

Responding to literature through writing presents additional learning opportunities that encourage children to reflect on what they read (see Chapter 3).

Free Writing

Children welcome the chance to choose what they write and how they will present it (see Chapter 3).

Proofreading

Writing involves more than just putting pen to paper. It also means getting a message across. Children can begin using proofreading skills from the very first time they write (see Chapter 5).

Spelling

How children learn about spelling is very much dependent on how it is presented. Setting targets is one way of providing a purpose while making spelling fun at the same time.

Class Spelling Target

Everyone can work together to explore unique patterns and irregularities in language. Regardless of ability, every child can benefit from focusing on a class target (see Chapter 6).

Group Spelling Target

Sometimes a few children need to look at the same words or a particular area of spelling, such as endings or blends. Planning group targets ensures that these children get that assistance (see Chapter 6).

Passing Spelling Target

It's fun to look at words and talk about them. Passing targets encourage children to word watch (see Chapter 6).

Individual Spelling Target

To ensure that every child works with words that he or she needs and uses, the individual target program focuses on words from each child's own writing (see Chapter 7).

Chapter Two

SETTING UP YOUR CLASSROOM FOR SUCCESS

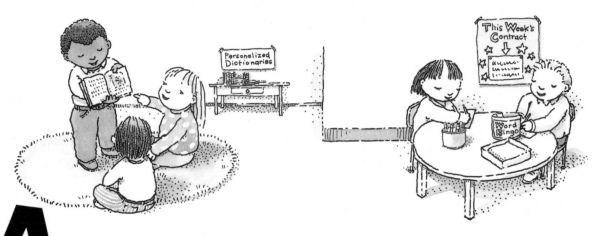

A classroom that is stimulating, rich in resources, supportive, and immerses children in print...A teacher who demonstrates language use, encourages children to experiment, and responds positively to children's language attempts...Children who are encouraged to take responsibility, use resources, experiment with language, and create further learning opportunities, are all part of an exciting world for teaching and learning.

For children to see connections between spelling and the printed word, they need to have many samples and supporting materials to guide them in language experiences. They need a teacher who can guide them and model reading, writing, and speaking skills. The classroom, teacher, and children described above combine to create this kind of meaningful and positive environment where real learning, including spelling, takes place.

Environmental stimuli, useful resources, and stimulating activities give teachers opportunities to share their knowledge about language with students, while children with confidence and enthusiasm can experiment with and increase their knowledge about language. This enthusiasm and practical application helps ensure that spelling, too, is seen as a very real and necessary skill.

Creating such an environment requires preparation, organization, and planning. In this chapter you'll find a range of resources for establishing an exciting and appropriate environment for you and your students, including:

- classroom features,
- classroom materials,
- individual materials, and
- other extras.

Of course, the most important aspect of any classroom is that it belongs to the children, too.

CLASSROOM FEATURES

First impressions of any classroom can indicate a teacher's approach. For example, seating arranged so that children face each other encourages group discussion and "talking for learning." A room that has student work on display suggests that children's efforts are valued and encouraged. Following are some suggestions you might like to try in your classroom.

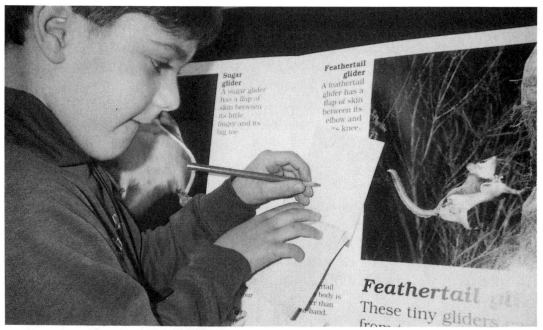

Using resources — a factual text — to find a word needed for unit writing.

Working Areas

Children's tables are arranged so that everyone is part of a working group. Each working area has a storage tub for writing implements and one for personal stationery. There is space around the tables for children to move freely and for the teacher to rove.

Quiet Reading Area

A class library offers opportunities for children to read a variety of materials. Class publications, factual texts, picture books, big books, rhyme and riddle books, magazines, school bulletins, comics, postcards, and hobby books are just some of the kinds of literature you might make available.

Discussion Den

This floor area has sufficient space for the entire class to sit together. It's a place where whole-class, small-group, and individual conferences take place. This is a place for share times, read-alouds, listening activities, and game playing. To put it simply, it's a class meeting place.

Computer Corner

A computer is available for children to work individually, in pairs, or in small groups. If students are using the computer for "writing," you might keep some spelling reference materials here for easy access.

Interest Areas

Interest areas support units of work students are studying. A jigsaw table, a life-cycle area, a garden, a shop, and model-flying machines are examples of some you might use. Interest areas are constantly changing as instructional focuses shift.

Display Area

This area includes books, posters, models, and equipment that support integrated units in progress. Children can bring materials from home to share with the class and add to the display area.

CLASS MATERIALS

Many of the resources in your classroom are potential tools for sharing knowledge about language and spelling. You can help your students make the most of these materials by modeling how to use them. At the same time, you'll encourage the inquisitive and enthusiastic learners in your students.

Labeling

All equipment, cupboards, interest areas, and containers are labeled so that children can read labels, see correct spellings, and see language being used for a real purpose. Everything is labeled so that children know where to find materials and have easy access to equipment they require. Children might enjoy helping you write these labels.

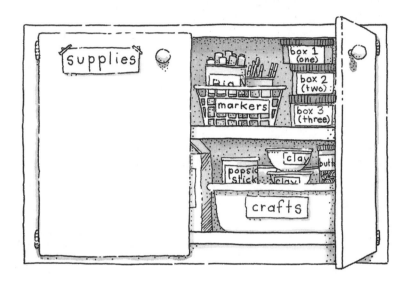

Containers and baskets for writing implements are labeled with numerals and words.

Information is added to storage equipment rather than just single labels.

Storage

The classroom equipment that children use is housed in tubs, boxes, and other containers that are within their reach. Many of the containers, such as ice-cream containers, food tins, and shoe boxes, might come from children's homes. All storage equipment should be labeled.

Posters and Charts

A combination of the following charts around the room helps create a colorful, stimulating environment:

- commercially produced and teacher-created charts supporting current units of work;
- charts listing commonly used words and other high-frequency words such as days of the week, months of the year, numerals in words, children's names; and
- charts representing specific studies within units of work.

Children can add to charts around the room by collecting information and creating their own posters.

Children refer to charts with high-frequency words for their writing.

A beanstalk is used to display ideas from the story "Jack and the Beanstalk."

Displays

Some displays are permanent and remain in the classroom throughout the year. These might include classroom rules and procedures, a monitor's or class-helper's board, and a timetable that shows group activities. Other displays continually change to suit a current unit of work.

Children's Work

Children's work is constantly on display and always changing. Art work, projects, writing forms, publications, and notices are just some of the work that can be read and shared.

Variety in Fonts

Posters, charts, labels, and displays in the room can be presented in a variety of ways to ensure children are able to identify letters and words written in different styles. Print, modern cursive script, typewritten, lower-case, upper-case, newspaper texts, computer type, and paper cutout letters are examples of print children can read.

Today's Busy Worker

A permanent display for the day's "busy worker" is a way to recognize individual children for their efforts. You might display a piece of work well done or a message about a child who has worked well. This changes daily. Children will look forward each day to reading about a class member recognized as a special achiever.

Work well done is displayed for the entire class to celebrate.

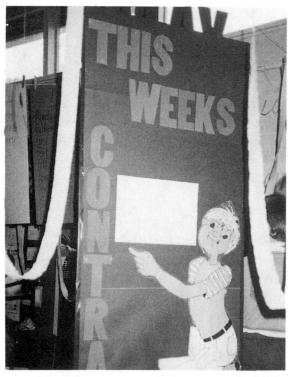

Displaying contracts promotes independence and the opportunity to use language for gathering information.

This Week's Contract

This display shows children what has to be completed during independent working times throughout the week. Tasks are varied each week and may include:

- a sample activity to be completed;
- a list of tasks;
- a special message such as "Play with a new friend" or "Have a giggle today";
- the title, author, and illustrator of a book that they might read or browse through; or
- searches such as "Find as many words that begin with 'C' and add them to our 'C' chart."

Alphabet Cards

Small cards with letters of the alphabet written on them are readily available for children to use. They can make their words, create word steps, and put words into alphabetical order.

Children are encouraged to use alphabet cards for learning individual target words.

100 Most-Used Words Mini-Mats

With the help of your students create a list of the 100 Most-Used Words or use the one on page 111. Paste lists onto cards and cover with contact paper. Students can take these mats to writing locations at any time and refer to them easily instead of having to look up at a chart above eye level. An alternative is to make a copy of the 100 Most-Used Words and affix one to every table.

Handwriting Strips

A strip of the handwriting style students use is fixed to each table to assist with letter formation. It is also a reference for putting letters and words into alphabetical order.

The A to Z of Writing

This display suggests a variety of writing styles such as recipes, lists, letters, articles, jokes, nonsense rhymes, and reports to encourage children to vary their individual writing.

A	Awards, Articles	**N**	Newspapers, Notes
B	Bedtime stories, Brain teasers	**O**	Opinions
C	Cartoons, Chants,Cards	**P**	Poetry, Plays, Pantomimes, Puzzles
D	Definitions, Diaries	**Q**	Quizzes, Quotes
E	Endings, Explanations	**R**	Recipes, Rhymes, Riddles
F	Fairy tales, Fables	**S**	Signs, Songs, Stories
G	Graffiti, Greetings	**T**	Titles, Tales
H	Headlines	**U**	Urgent messages
I	Invitations, Instructions	**V**	Verse
J	Jokes	**W**	Warnings
K	Knowledge	**X**	eXciting stories
L	Lists, Letters	**Y**	Yarns
M	Magazines, Mysteries, Messages	**Z**	Zzzzz—Boring stories that send you to sleep

Dictionaries/Thesauruses/Word Books

If a class set is available, keep a dictionary at each table for easy reference. Alternatively you can create a resource center that offers a wide variety of dictionaries and thesauruses. Other useful books include those with collections of words with common themes like "My first action words" or "At the supermarket" books.

Topic Charts/Topic Tins/Topic Books

As you create new word charts for work in progress, you can transfer information from charts to cards for a topic tin or to pages in a topic book. Children can help by reading words from the chart and providing appropriate names for the tins or books. You can label and store these resources on a shelf for easy access. I found that if children are part of the process then they have an easier time referring to the tins or books to find words they're looking for. Some books and tins you might want to create include words relating to a specific theme, words with a common pattern, alternative words, and sound symbol words.

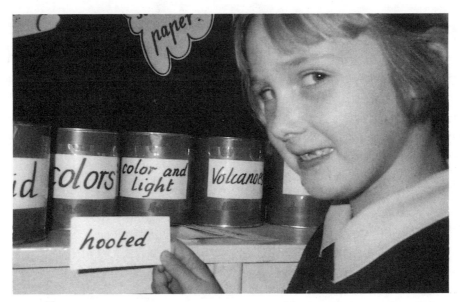

Topic tins are a great resource for children. Alternative words are often referred to for children's writing.

Alphabet Charts

Cut out each letter of the alphabet on large cards and paste onto cupboard doors or the windows. Throughout the year add words that children learn, words of interest, and new words in proximity to the appropriate letter. Children can refer to these charts and take pride in making additions to them.

Commercial Games

A range of games is available commercially to encourage children to learn about words. Some of these include Scrabble™, Junior Scrabble™, Up Words™, Boggle™, and Scattergories™.

Class Games

Games you can make to promote spelling skills include Word-Bank Bingo, Spell of the Century, word finds, crosswords, alpha names, alpha sorts, and Challenge. (See Chapter 8 for instructions on making these games.)

INDIVIDUAL MATERIALS

Your language and spelling program will require materials for students' individual use. You'll find it extremely valuable if these materials assist you in program planning and evolution, too. Try using some of the following.

Writing File

Children should have one file that contains two manila folders. One folder contains current works and the second folder contains ideas, other drafts, revised editions of work, and so on. By keeping these two folders children can more easily identify their current working document and you can more immediately reference children's work in progress and their previous efforts for evaluation purposes.

Word Banks

These are containers children use to store the individual target words they are learning each week (see Chapter 8). They are small enough to fit into their tubs (margarine tubs, mini bins, stock cube containers, and mini boxes). When children are working with their individual target words there is no need to refer to individual dictionaries or Spelling-Tries Sheets. All they require are their word banks.

Containers with lids are the most practical holders for word banks.

Target Challenge Booklets

Children record their weekly challenge of individual target words in these booklets (see Chapter 8). You can make them with students at the beginning of the year and use them to record a full year's words. By recording the date on each challenge, the booklet serves as an evaluation tool for both you and the child.

Word Saver

The individual target words that each child learns from week to week go into their word savers. This becomes a collection of words they have learned throughout the year which can be used for sorting, alphabetizing, and playing word games.

Individual Dictionaries

Children use this book to record all words from their Spelling-Tries Sheet (see Chapter 5) and any other words they require throughout the year. This way it doesn't matter if children can spell certain words independently—those words are in their dictionaries to refer to in future writing sessions. Another good reference is to put the 100 Most-Used Words inside the front cover. Commercially produced dictionaries, index books, or exercise books with a page for each letter can all serve as individual dictionaries.

Individual dictionaries can be made from any blank book.

Personal Diaries

Children can record thoughts, ideas, and observations in personal diaries. Students who want a response from you can place their diaries in a Diary Deposit Tub. Children are encouraged to write as often as they can in their diaries.

OTHER EXTRAS

Here are a few suggestions for those bits and pieces that help pull your writing program together. Keeping extra supplies on hand can save you valuable time in the future.

Date Stamp

A date stamp comes in handy for dating writing drafts, spelling tries, and other documents children produce. This assists with evaluation during the year.

Draft Stamp

This stamp identifies work in progress. This is particularly useful when children take their work home. Parents recognize that it is a working document by the draft stamp.

Mini Cards

Make mini cards readily available for writing individual words for word banks, words for topic tins, and words for classroom lists. These cards are about 1 1/2 inches by 4 inches. They are also useful when children want to write down words from charts, big books, and displays to use in their writing. It's easier to take mini cards back to their work areas and copy the required words into their writing than refer to a chart above eye level.

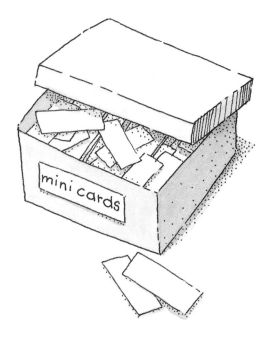

A supply of mini cards is always at hand for children to use. They are also useful for the teacher to jot down words when children don't have time to use spelling tries.

Topic Books

Blank books that have been sliced in half or thirds are handy to use for topic books.

Class-Made Booklets

Have a collection of booklets with covers and internal blank pages available to make class topic books and individual books for children.

Spelling-Tries Sheets

Children use these forms when attempting to fix the spelling of words from their individual writing. Each completed sheet is dated and kept in children's writing files for evaluation purposes. *(For a copy of this sheet see page 106.)*

Writing File Storage

An archive box is ideal for storing children's writing files.

Writing files are accessible for children at all times.
It is handy to store each file in alphabetical order.

Easel

A readily available easel with large sheets clipped to it comes in handy for small-group discussions, brain-storming exercises, wall stories, and other modeled writing experiences.

Spare Paper Box

Place old notices, activity sheets, computer paper, and other used paper in a box for recycling. Children can use this paper for writing drafts, playing hangman, "Look, Say, Cover, Write, Check" exercises, and free-writing sessions.

Children are encouraged to use a variety of writing paper for drafting, free writing, and publishing.

Diary Deposit

Children who want responses to their individual diary entries can place their books in the Diary Deposit Tub. After reading and responding, you can return the diaries to children's tubs or lockers.

Chapter Three

WRITING FOR ALL OCCASIONS

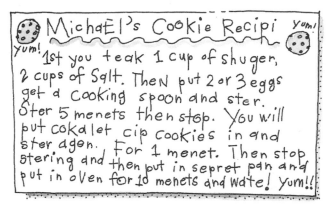

Spelling and writing go hand in hand. When children want to convey messages through writing, they are automatically in a position to use knowledge they have about spelling. In other words, real writing purposes gives spelling meaning.

With this in mind, the types of words children use will depend largely on the writing experiences they are involved in. If a writing program is based solely on story writing, then children might confidently use such words as *once*, *upon*, *happily*, *ever*, and *after*. But children engaged in completing reports on a science experiment might not find these words so important. Instead, they might attempt to use words like *equipment*, *hypothesize*, *predict*, and *change*.

By broadening children's experiences, many writing opportunities find a natural place in the integrated curriculum and provide children with a meaningful context to learn new words and spelling strategies. I find that this is best accomplished in my writing program by planning around four areas. This structure helps me be sure that children have every opportunity to experience the many writing styles available to them.

The four areas I plan for are:

- free writing
- unit writing
- literature writing
- personal writing

Each week, children have the opportunity to write in all of these areas. Sometimes one writing task will last for a period of weeks such as the development of a research topic during integrated studies. In this case, children draft, rewrite, research, proofread, and publish their work. While carrying out these writing processes, children are able to use the skills they acquire during formal modeling, conferencing, or other related sessions. Rehearsing spelling strategies is a major part of these processes (see Chapter 5).

Other times a writing task may consist of just a conceptual idea, such as preparing a description for a photographic display. In this case the children may be responsible for drafting their ideas while I attend to proofreading for spelling, grammar, and punctuation. Children are now able to move directly to publishing their work. On these occasions, you can still encourage children to use research, word-attack, and proofreading skills as part of the overall writing task. So in fact, what you'll be doing is ensuring that writing skills and spelling strategies automatically become part of the writing process regardless of the task length or expected outcome.

Throughout the year students will complete many writing tasks and publish a wide range of materials as a part of the class program. For individual writing tasks such as fictional stories, they may only publish six pieces for the year. It is unrealistic to try formal conferencing and ongoing development with every piece of writing a child begins. By focusing on several specific areas, you can plan what and how much skill development is approached through each writing task.

As each child establishes new proofreading and word-attack skills, encourage them to incorporate the new knowledge into every writing activity attempted. Beginning writers will use proofreading strategies they are familiar with while more confident writers will also use strategies such as spelling tries (see Chapter 5). Each child brings existing spelling skills and repertoire to the writing experience, creating opportunities to build a spelling program around their attempts.

Following is a closer look at each of the four writing areas. Once you're familiar with the opportunities they present, you'll want to explore how proofreading and spelling fit in (see Chapter 4).

FREE WRITING

Free writing time gives children opportunities to write in any style they like, such as stories, letters to friends, invitations, jokes, plays, and poetry. Children are not expected to have a conference with each free writing composition unless they choose to. The main purpose of this writing session is to give children time to play with language. They are free to decide how they will use this writing time.

Sometimes a child may decide to work on an ongoing composition, while other times the session may be spent writing notes to a friend or designing birthday cards. The opportunity for children to select their own writing styles and purposes is what counts. This time also encourages children to use known spelling strategies and make approximations about unknown words.

Throughout the year you can introduce and model different writing styles so that your students have a broad repertoire to choose from. Displays around the room, suggesting different styles and various models of each, help children select and work with their individual compositions.

You can support free writing in your classroom by offering a variety of resources such as a graffiti board, a letter box, recycled envelopes, charts displaying writing styles, draft paper, and a diary deposit box. Children can keep their free writing pieces in writing folders. Other writing pieces can be

given to friends, put in the letter box, placed on the graffiti board, or taken home. At the end of each free writing session, invite children to share their work with the entire class or small groups.

The letter box is used frequently by the children, particularly during free writing time. It's fun to choose a postman each day to clear the mail.

UNIT WRITING

All writing in this area is centered around integrated units of study and includes a range of writing styles for different purposes. There are many opportunities for children to write independently as well as in cooperative groups. There are also many occasions when the entire class works together to create a manuscript.

Some unit writing tasks you might introduce to your students include:

Wall stories	Contents for this may come from shared experiences, excursions, or factual information the class gathers.
Letters	Write thank-you letters following excursions or visits from guest speakers, formal letters or notices when planning outings, and personal letters for family and friends.
Graphs	Gather explanations and summaries of information and present as supporting information on a graph.
Directions	Gather simple recipes in a class or individual recipe book. Students, for example, can explain how to grow herbs in written form.
Reports	Report outcomes of science experiments, excursions, or shared experiences.
Projects	Present information about a specific topic in book, brochure, poster, or chart form.
Focus questions	Note information about research topics before, during, and after a unit of work.

Children are involved in gathering data and preparing a graph for interpretation. Therefore, the information is meaningful to them.

During these unit writing sessions, encourage children to use spelling strategies they have developed during other writing sessions. As they work at their individual levels, offer praise for all attempts made.

Your purpose for unit writing will determine what kind of individual conferences take place. For writing exercises, you can address content, proofreading skills, spelling, and other writing conventions in individual conferences. If unit writing tasks are for quick publications such as class books, thank-you letters, or displays, you probably won't spend as much time on the writing and spelling strategies mentioned above.

In this case, for example, you might write correct spellings so that children can move straight to writing final copy. If you are typing final copy for a child, you might

Children work in pairs to rewrite and publish familiar books.

take notes for your own information but choose not to discuss spelling in detail in order to speed up the process. Some unit writing tasks, such as cooperative group focus questions, won't be published at all. The purpose of this writing exercise is to gather information; therefore, you might naturally focus less on spelling.

The most important thing to remember while working with unit writing is that the objective of the writing task needs to be clearly defined. Once the objective is set, the skills and understandings to be addressed will be clear, and you won't waste valuable time trying to include all writing and spelling conventions in every piece of unit writing.

LITERATURE WRITING

There are many opportunities for children to write as a result of literature shared in the classroom. These writing tasks differ in purpose and style, too. They also vary from whole-class to small-group and individual writing tasks.

Literature writing sessions provide time for children to respond to the literature that they read. Sample literature writing tasks include:

Predictions	Speculating about the contents of a book by looking at the front cover or reading the blurb. Predicting the ending of a story. These predictions are recorded.
Descriptions	Compiling portraits of characters from books.
Sequencing	Writing summaries of stories, creating story maps, and rewriting stories.
Recording	Writing about favorite characters and events of a story.
Interpreting	Changing the text from a story, using illustrations as a guide.
Cloze	Writing cloze exercises using a novel, factual text, or picture book.
Entertainment	Writing stories and poems to share with others.

Literature writing sessions incorporate spelling strategies that are used in all other writing sessions.

Recreating dust jackets of a favorite book includes writing a blurb for the story. Spelling is practiced during the writing process. It's a great alternative to the book report.

PERSONAL WRITING

Personal writing gives children an opportunity to record feelings, observations, and outcomes of their personal lives. Children can date and compile this writing in personal books.

Established writers can record personal writing in "individual diaries." These diaries do not require compulsory responses from you. However, children who would like responses can place their diaries in a Diary Deposit Tub (see page 24). The emphasis for diary entries is on children's thoughts. Therefore, you won't be concerned with written conventions and spelling as teaching objectives. You can, however, include correct conventions and spellings in your responses to further reinforce correct spelling, grammar, and punctuation as exemplified on the following page.

Dear Diary,

On sunday I had my frand owvr my hose At the moning Sonoco and me had a moning fest.

Eri.

Dear Eri,

Wow! A morning feast with Sonoco sounds like the perfect way to spend Sunday morning. Does your friend come over to your house every weekend?

Diary.

For beginning and reluctant writers, personal diaries are difficult to use to their fullest potential as children's intended messages aren't always clear to the reader. In this case, you might use personal writing as a framework for developing a greater understanding about language and spelling. This is outlined in the following chapter.

Chapter Four

A WRITING PROGRAM FOR BEGINNING AND RELUCTANT WRITERS

Language learning develops from the beginning of a child's life. Children learn to speak by constantly hearing language, using language, and receiving feedback about all attempts they make. The same thing occurs with children beginning to read and write. They need to constantly interact with the written word and use language from their own world to develop greater understandings about literacy.

I use the personal writing model described in Chapter 3 in my classroom to develop an individual writing program for beginning and reluctant writers. This program is designed to cater to the needs of every child, regardless of ability. Each child's own language is used as the framework for further language work throughout the program. By using this individual program I am able to help every child build up spelling strategies, word-attack skills, and other language knowledge at the right time for their needs.

The Individual Writing Program introduces beginning and reluctant writers to using whole, meaningful language so that they have the confidence to write in the other three areas described in Chapter 3 (free writing, unit writing, and literature writing).

This program also acts as a prerequisite to the Individual Spelling Program (see Chapter 7).

Program Outline

The Individual Writing Program occurs over a one-week period with a different activity occurring each day. Even children at the scribble stage can complete each activity throughout the week. The program begins with children completing a piece of writing on the first day. They use this one piece for the remainder of the week in all other activities. The program concludes with children publishing their original pieces of writing.

This program continues from week to week until children are able to move on to the personal writing described in Chapter 3.

You may read through this chapter and think that you'll never find the time to individualize your writing program. It does take time and effort to get it working smoothly. But you'll find that your students are quick to understand the tasks involved and the routines that occur. Before long, with a little patience, they'll be able to work more independently and efficiently on program components. Best of all, you and your students will see great achievements as a result of your efforts.

The outline on the next page describes the procedure for the first day's activity and the approximate time you'll want to set aside for each task. Remember to keep in mind your own organizational strategies and adapt these procedures to suit your own needs and timetable.

DAY 1: CREATING A PIECE OF WRITING

The first session is a whole language time where speaking, listening, modeled writing, conferencing, and reading takes place. At the end of this first session, every child will have a piece of writing to use for the remainder of the week. Below is the schedule I use on the first day.

SCHEDULE FOR DAY 1	
1. Setting the Mood The entire class shares a common experience in preparation for writing.	**15 minutes**
2. Discussion Time Children share their thoughts and ideas with the class.	**5 minutes**
3. Class Conference A writing demonstration points out the many conventions and strategies children can use for their own writing.	**10 minutes**
4. Personal Writing/Individual Conferences Children work on their own writing and other language tasks. They have an individual conference about their writing.	**50 minutes**
5. Share Time Children are encouraged to share their efforts with the class while other class members ask questions and congratulate individuals for all achievements.	**10 minutes**

Setting the Mood

At the beginning of each week the class shares a common experience, adventure, book, or reflections on a common topic. The idea behind this is to stimulate children's thoughts and provide some prewriting warm-ups such as thinking about ideas, sharing ideas, getting feedback, and developing the desire to write. Listed below are activities I've used to set the mood.

Shared Experiences: Our shared experiences relate to integrated unit being studied. For instance when doing a unit of work on "Shops and Shopping" we went for a walk to the local shopping center to observe the types of shops there. For a unit on "Our Body" we had the opportunity to see a model of a torso showing the internal organs and how they fit together. Our unit of work on "Caterpillars and Life Cycles" included creating an environment for silk worms and our "Growing and Changing" unit included a visit from a mother with her newborn baby. We watched the baby being bathed, changed, and fed. Each shared experience not only provides a stepping stone for writing, it also leads to many other valuable activities for the week.

Our shopping journey led to the study of the 'sh' blend.

Shared Adventures: Our shared adventures are all about fantasy and fun. Sometimes we have a special day such as Tie Day where all the children wear special ties and explain why they chose them. Other adventures include traveling to magical places under the sea or to magical forests. These adventures take place in the classroom or in other locations around the school. There are endless opportunities for children to use their imaginations and ideas.

Shared Books: Sharing books is always a part of our integrated units or literature focus. During this time lots of discussion takes place about the book. Sometimes a book may even lead to a quick adventure or experience. For example, on my students' first day of school, we read *Rosie's Walk* by Pat Hutchins (Macmillan, 1968). Afterwards, we took a walk around the school grounds, doing all the things Rosie did: going up, down, around, over, and under. Next, we wrote our own version called *Kinder L's Walk* —our very first class book and publication.

Common Topics: Some prewriting sessions are opportunities to share personal experiences about common topics. These might include discussions about what children did on the weekend, parties, a favorite toy, or even what they have in their lunch boxes. These common topics give every child the chance to draw on personal experiences from their own world. Whatever stimulus is presented, each prewriting session gives all children the opportunity to participate.

Discussion Time

After setting the scene with a shared experience, book, or topic, children move into small groups of their choice to discuss thoughts, opinions, feelings, and experiences. They actively listen to others, speak to others, ask questions, construct their thoughts, and gather feedback about their ideas or experiences—all in preparation for their personal writing. The class then comes together and several children share their experiences with the entire class.

Class Conference

A modeled writing session, presented by myself or one of the children, follows our discussions. The idea behind the modeled writing is to demonstrate the way thoughts and ideas can be recorded as writing.

During this time, I discuss learning outcomes, going into greater detail with one specific outcome that children will develop in their individual writing.

A Sample Class Conference

Let's say I plan to write "On Sunday night I went to a Chinese restaurant with my cousin. We had garlic prawns and fried rice. It tasted delicious." I might use the sentence to introduce spelling skills such as: capital letters, the *w* letter and sound, full stops, the *th* blend and the use of spaces between words. I might select one in particular, such as using spaces, to have children focus on in their own writing. These skills, called *passing targets* and specific learning outcomes, are discussed in more detail in Chapter 5.

The conference begins with telling the children what I have decided to write. I explain how I am writing the information and I ask questions of them during the modeling. For example:

> *The first word is* **On***. I'm starting here on the left and I'm going to write across this way to the right. This word is at the start of the sentence so it must begin with a capital letter.*

I continue writing while discussing the following features:

- *We need to leave a space between each word.*
- *Some other words have capital letters, too. They're called proper nouns.*
- *I am at the end of the line, so I'm going back to the left and writing across to the right again.*
- *I'll see if the word* **with** *is on our word mat. Here it is. I'll copy the whole word.*

- *Look. The word **went** and the word **with** begin with the same letter.*
- *The word **cousin** is in our Family Word Book. I'll use that to help me spell it.*
- *This is the end of my sentence. A full stop has to go here.*
- ***Restaurant** is a tricky word. I'll write it the way I think it is spelled and check it later.*

On Sunday night I went
to a Chinese restaurant
with my cousin.

At the same time I would be asking questions, too:

- *I've written **On Sunday night I** what word comes next?*
- *What is going to come between each word?*
- *What letter does **went** and **with** begin with?*
- *What sound does the letter make?*
- *What other words start with the same sound?*
- *What letter do you think the word **cousin** begins with?*
- *What do I need at the end of my sentence?*

As I continue writing, I continue to go back and reread what I have written, ensuring I run my fingers under each word as I read it. When the writing is completed I invite children to read it with me while I point to each word. Then, individual children can volunteer to read my work. The conference concludes with emphasizing "spaces between words" (the specific learning outcome), reminding children to use spaces during their writing.

Personal Writing

Children are now ready to do their own writing in their personal writing books. I divide reluctant and beginning writers' personal writing books into four sections for starters, with each section representing a different purpose for each activity. At the end of the week the entire double page will serve as an extremely valuable evaluation tool for both you and your students.

As students become more confident in their writing and show signs of developing as writers, their books no longer need to be divided. At this point, children can move out of the Individual Writing Program and into the "individual target" spelling program (see Chapter 8), and their personal writing in individual diaries.

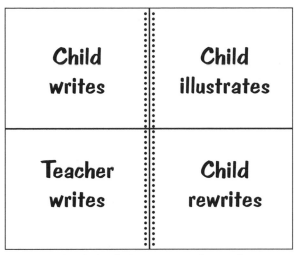

Child writes	Child illustrates
Teacher writes	Child rewrites

A sample left-right page of a reluctant and beginning writer's book.

During personal writing time, encourage children to address the "specific learning outcome." When you spot a child using it (for example, using a space between words), offer praise. This provides positive feedback to the child using the skill and is an additional reminder for other children to focus their attention on the learning outcome as well.

(Entry is written at the top left-hand side of page.)

MY brotHEr es
sc e l w Lk
+ Gf HM A btD.

My brother is sick and I would like to give him a birthday.

This sample shows that Kirsten used spaces in her writing. The spaces between each word assist the reader in understanding her spelling attempts. It is also clear that she understands and uses two other incidental skills I previously modeled:

1. She used the Same Family Words Book to find the word *brother* for her writing.
2. She put a full stop at the end of her sentence.

Individual Conferences

While my students are involved in their personal writing, I use this time to carry out individual conferences with the children. During each individual conference, I focus on all of the writing successes that each child achieves. Regardless of the stage the child is at, there is always something positive to recognize. Even children who illustrate instead of write can be congratulated on their drawings and the way they describe them.

At individual conference time I also discuss a number of relevant issues such as the way letters represent sounds in words, the evidence of common blends, or anything else specific to that writing. This encourages children's word watching and awareness of the appropriate use of written language.

Finally, I write the child's intended message saying things like "Terrific!

Would does begin with *w*. Here's how the whole word is spelled." In this way, the child is getting positive feedback for all attempts and also sees the correct spelling written. I write the correct spellings in the bottom left-hand box below the child's message. By writing the intended message in a separate location, students can refer to the correct model for the additional activities through the week. The attempts each child makes are not defaced or altered in any way. Therefore, their original efforts remain unchanged and become evaluation pieces. Finally, the child is able to read the entire correct model.

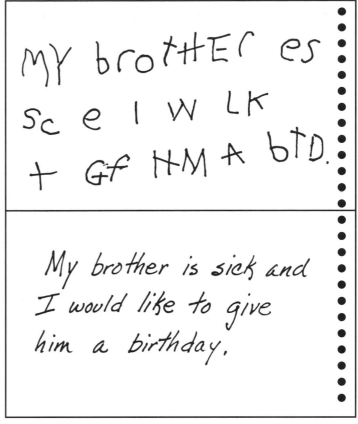

Teacher creates a model by writing at the bottom left-hand corner what student intended to write at the top left-hand corner.

Share Time

At the end of the session I invite several children to share their work with the class. At this time the class acts as an audience while the individual child reads his or her writing to the group. The audience can ask questions about the content of the text.

Children in the audience are then invited to point out specific positive points about the writing. This teacher-directed discussion gives further positive feedback for the writer and the audience. Sample feedback you might model for your students includes:

> Teacher: John knows what to use at the start of the sentence. Can someone share with the class what John did?
> Response: He used a capital letter.
> Teacher: What letter did John use at the beginning of the word *Mom*?
> Response: *M*.
> Teacher: Who can think of some other words that have the same beginning sound?

I PW MKST.

IGOZMB•

≢ᴚ∃ɗꜰⱢⴆꜱᴣi

one
two
three
four
tive
six
seven
eight
nine
ten

Day 2 to Day 5

For the remainder of the week children complete a range of activities using the correct models of their intended messages. Regardless of their original attempts, every child has a correct model to work from. Some of the week's activities are completed in the remaining sections of students' personal writing books. These activities are designed to develop children's awareness and skills in:

- written conventions,
- correct spelling,
- conventional handwriting,
- expanding on original ideas,
- sight vocabulary,
- text sequencing, and
- publishing.

By the end of the week students have a complete page of writing that shows their efforts and achievements. It's especially rewarding to review children's work after a few weeks to see the progress they've made. It really is a sight to behold.

Each session (Days 2-5) follows the format described below.

SCHEDULE FOR DAYS 2-5	
1. Tuning In	**5 minutes**
A whole class language activity such as shared reading, rhymes, chants, discussions, or a language game sets the tone for a positive language environment.	
2. Class Conference	**5 minutes**
The written sample from the previous day is shared and discussed. The new task is modeled.	
3. Individual Working Time	**15 minutes**
Each child works on their individual text completing the tasks discussed during the class conference. The teacher walks around the room conferencing with students.	
4. Share Time	**5 minutes**
Children have an opportunity to share and discuss achievements from the session.	

DAY 2: EXPANDING ON IDEAS

This session focuses on the ability to expand on original ideas and thoughts. It shows children that written information can be developed further through discussion, illustrations, and additional text.

The writing sample I modeled from on Day 1 is discussed giving more information about the subject. For example, I might add:

> "At the restaurant there were lots of other people there. Some people were celebrating a birthday too. The restaurant was called Chopsticks. It's my favorite Chinese restaurant." Children are encouraged to ask questions about the passage to elicit more information.

Next, decide how to illustrate the passage. Quickly explain and draw the illustration. In the top right-hand section of the personal book, label parts of the illustration for additional information.

Children now complete the same task with their passages.

DAY 3: REWRITING THE PASSAGE

This activity focuses on rewriting the passage by using the correct model as a guide. Children rewrite their intended messages and read them once completed. This gives them an opportunity to practice correct letter formation while using the correct model as a guide. This activity is also the first step to developing proofreading and spelling strategies (see Chapter 5). This task is completed on the bottom right-hand side of the personal writing book.

As you create the modeled passage:
- reread the text,
- run a finger under each word before writing it,
- discuss the shape of the letters,
- emphasize spaces between words,
- comment on interesting letter and sound combinations, and
- emphasize capital letters, full stops, and other writing conventions.

Demonstrate that the text is written correctly and reread the passage. Children then read the new version as you run a finger under each word.

Children now complete the same task with their passages.

I went to the shops.	I went to the shops.

DAY 4: SENTENCE CONSTRUCTION

This activity uses sentence strips to focus on the sequencing of words in the passage. It aims at distinguishing between sentences, words, and letters, and focuses on aspects of each.

First, write *your* modeled passage on a sentence strip. Read the passage from the sentence strip while running a finger under each word. Invite children to read the sentence. Count the number of words in the passage, pointing to each word as you do so.

On	Sunday	night	I	went	to	a	Chinese	restaurant.

Next, cut the sentence strip into words. Jumble up the words and use the passage from the personal book to recreate the sample. Invite a couple of children to try.

On Sunday night I went to a Chinese restaurant.

Other activities you can try with *your* sentence strip (and later with students' personal writing) include:

- hiding a word from the passage (students guess the hidden word);
- counting the number of letters in some words;
- looking at the initial letter or sound at the beginning of some words;
- looking at the final letter or sound in some words;
- looking at interesting letter blends;
- discussing other words with the same sound or letter combination;
- sharing alternative words.

Finally, paste your sentence strip over your original modeled sample on the bottom left-hand section of the personal writing book. At this time, discuss the sequencing of the sentence along with some words, letters, and sound combinations.

Children can now complete the same task with their passages. At this point every child will have his or her own sentence strips. (It helps to prepare the sentence strips for students in advance.) When handing out sentence strips, try finding owners by asking questions about each child's passage rather than reading it completely. By doing this, children will have to listen carefully and focus on the content of their passage rather than identifying their own passage by rote reading.

DAY 5: PUBLISHING

This final session demonstrates the variety of ways in which children's writing may be published. You might demonstrate a different publishing style or a specific aspect of publishing each week. Start by copying the correct model (a rewritten version of the passage on a sentence strip or the sample in the personal writing book) on a separate piece of paper. Suggestions for publishing include:

- giving the passage a title;
- creating a border for the passage;
- using the passage to create a display;
- putting the passage in a self-addressed envelope to send to a special family member;

- collecting each child's publication to create a class book for the week;
- compiling collections of individual children's work into books;
- including a contents page, title page, page numbers, and an "about the author" section;
- turning the passage into a cartoon or comic strip;
- typing the passage rather than rewriting it; and
- doing an art activity to illustrate the passage a different way.

Children are now ready to publish their passages.

A Sample of work from one week's activities.

- Child writes in the top left-hand box.
- Teacher scribes child's attempt in bottom left-hand box.
- Child illustrates writing in top right-hand box.
- Child rewrites text in bottom right-hand box, using teacher model.

Moving Beyond the Individual Writing Program

The Individual Writing Program described in this chapter is designed to support beginning or reluctant writers. The idea behind dividing the book pages into four sections is to encourage children to use real language and develop their understandings about how written language works through their own thoughts and ideas. At no time should children be inhibited by the four sections.

If children want to write more, by all means encourage them. But ask that the same activities be completed. For children who are still beginning writers, you might suggest using a portion of their passages for the remaining activities (Days 2-5) instead of using their entire pieces.

As children become more confident and able writers they no longer require their entire works to be rewritten for them. At this point, you can encourage children to develop additional writing and spelling strategies. The following chapter describes steps for introducing proofreading and spelling techniques to these children.

Chapter Five

THE SPELLING CONFERENCE
Introducing Proofreading Strategies

As you see your students gradually taking more responsibility for what they are writing, you can apply the same philosophy to their attempts at spelling and proofreading. Spelling conferences are one way to help students achieve success with this goal. These conferences encourage children as they use newly acquired skills for further learning and assist them in understanding the connections between each writing experience.

Spelling conferences focus on building word-attack skills, word knowledge, and proofreading strategies. By gradually introducing proofreading skills to children in their conferences, each new skill becomes a building block for independence in the writing process. Because children work from their own individual drafts as they conference, there is purpose and meaning in the skills they are developing.

I have found that by working through four stages in the proofreading stage, children have a greater understanding of what is required. Stage one begins with the teacher rewriting all of the child's intended message. This is the same procedure as set out in the beginning writer's program (see Chapter 4).

The remaining three stages gradually decrease the teacher's scribing and increase the child's responsibility through the introduction of spelling tries, proofreading, and word-attack skills. Each stage has its own routine which helps children establish independence in working through the process. Some children can work through to stage four in their first year of school, while other children may need a few years to get there.

One important feature about these stages is that children take responsibility for ensuring all spelling is correct when they are publishing. But most importantly, every child is focusing on specific spelling needs as a result of their own writing.

Following is a detailed description of each stage, showing a logical progression of proofreading and spelling skills.

STAGE ONE:
THE CORRECT MODEL

Children in the first stage need to be encouraged to write independently and be congratulated for all efforts they make. This includes beginning writers' attempts, such as scribble, invented letters, illustrations only, print copied from the environment, as well as use of conventional letters.

In this stage of the spelling conference, you write the child's entire draft. The child can then use this model for reading, copying, and publishing. In other words, it doesn't matter what the child has attempted. Every child at this stage will have a complete correct model to work with. Celebrate all pen-to-paper action so children understand they are conveying messages with their efforts.

The most important thing to remember is that when children believe they are writers and readers, they have a solid beginning for growing as confident, competent writers and spellers.

The Spelling Conference (for Stage 1)

The following outline can help guide your spelling conferences:
1. The child reads the draft or discusses what he or she wanted to write. Sometimes at this stage a child may do an illustration instead of attempting to write. In this case, encourage the child to talk about the illustration.
2. Respond by congratulating the child for all attempts made.
3. Ask "How would you like me to write this?"
4. When you scribe the child's draft, it is important that you write below the child's efforts. This ensures that when the child is rereading and rewriting the text, the correct model is not confused with other attempts made. It also shows that the child's attempts are valued and have not been defaced in any way. Finally, the child's attempts are a sample of work achieved and are therefore a valuable evaluation tool.
5. As you scribe the child's draft, discuss each word and other conventions such as spaces between words, sounds that letters make, words with the same sound or initial letter, directionality, and full stops. You might also like to place a checkmark underneath each letter that the child uses correctly.
6. Read the text, running a finger underneath each word as it is read.
7. Read the text again, this time encouraging the child to read with you.
8. Invite the child to read the text alone, running a finger underneath each word as it is read.
9. A final positive response from you concludes the conference on a confident note.

Publishing

When children are rewriting or publishing their drafts, they can use the writing samples you scribe during the conferences. Every child, regardless of the original attempt, now has the opportunity to write a message using a conventional guide. While publishing, the child will be practicing correct letter formation at the same time.

I watched a video.	*I watched a video.*

STAGE TWO:
REPLACING CORRECT SPELLING

At this point children have a greater understanding of printed language. They refer to environmental print, write known words often, and attempt unfamiliar words with greater confidence.

When conferencing, there is no need to rewrite the child's entire text. Quite often the child will write several pages so it is not feasible to spend time rewriting everything. At this stage, too, the child knows what he or she writes and you can usually understand approximations of unfamiliar words.

Here, you will be introducing the child to the process of proofreading—or finding words that require fixing. As you move through the process, you'll congratulate efforts, underline misspelled words, discuss letter sound representations, and scribe correct spellings.

The child will now have the correct model of only the words that were misspelled. The child will use these words to replace the misspelled words in his or her publication but is not responsible for placing the correct spelling into the draft at this point.

On Saturday
I had a btday
paty. I had
los ov presnts.
I Lkit tem too.
and aftu the
paty sum ov
the pepl cam
to my plas.

birthday
party
lots
of
presents
liked
them
after
party
some
of
people
came
place

The Spelling Conference (for Stage 2)

1. The child reads the entire piece.
2. Congratulate the child for all words spelled correctly and for all other attempts made.
3. Read the text through with the child, stopping at words that need fixing.
4. As you reach a misspelled word, underline it and write the correct spelling at the end of the completed draft. It's easier for some children if you write the words in list form rather than writing them from left to right across the page. It is also easier if misspelled words are written in the order they appear. For example:
   *"Yes, **when** does begin with **w** and you can hear the **n** sound at the end of the word. Well done. There are some other letters needed in the middle to fix the word. These are **h** and **e**."*
   You might discuss the **wh** blend at this point, then write the word **when** below the text.
5. Continue with the remainder of the text.
6. Ask the child to reread the words that have been written correctly.
7. Finish the conference with a positive comment about the child's fine effort.

Publishing

The following procedure can guide children as they rewrite or publish their drafts. You might want to make a poster-size chart for easy reference.

1. Begin rewriting your draft.
2. Stop when you come to a word that is underlined.
3. Look at the words your teacher wrote to find the correct spelling for the underlined word.
4. Copy the correct word onto the publication.
5. Now underline this word to show that it has been used.
6. Continue rewriting.
7. Stop when you come to another word that is underlined.
8. Continue as before.

STAGE THREE:
SEARCHING FOR INCORRECT SPELLING

This stage introduces children to spelling tries at the completion of their drafts. They'll make connections between known words and words they would like to use. At this point, children can take responsibility for finding misspelled words and making attempts to fix them.

Encourage children at this stage to make approximations while writing, and promote the use of references as well. While writing, they may also refer to references in the room if they know where to find particular words. For example, children might find the word *Olympic* displayed on a brainstorming chart showing words related to the Olympic games. They might locate other words in word tins, word books, high-frequency charts, or individual dictionaries. Encourage word searching only if the children know where to find specific words. Searching for words at random wastes valuable writing time.

> the Olympic games wor opening I was 100
> uards away from the crtra cup I had
> a boe and aroe the frunt of the aroe
> was on fier. I shot the droe it went
> fluing to the cup it lita flam. I felt grate.

The child is satisfied with the draft and is ready to share it with the teacher.

Your involvement at this stage is to share word-attack strategies, proof-reading skills, and research skills. This stage also involves several conferences, each one lasting only a few minutes.

Conference 1

1. Share the draft with the child and congratulate all efforts made.
2. Ask the child to reread the draft independently and to underline any words that need fixing (see sample shown below).

the Olympic games wor opening I wasloo uards away from the _crtra_ cup I had a boe and _aroe_ the frunt of the _aroe_ was on fier. I shot the droe it went fluing to the cup it lita flam. I felt _grate_.

Conference 2

1. Congratulate the child for all proofreading efforts.
2. Underline any remaining words that are misspelled (as shown below), discussing why they need fixing and offering suggestions for achieving correct spellings. For example, "The word *flying* does have the *i* sound. This time the *i* sound is represented as it is in the word *my*. See if that helps you."
3. Give the child a Spelling-Tries Sheet (see page 106) for fixing misspelled words.

the Olympic games _wor_ opening I wasloo _uards_ away from the _crtra_ cup I had a _boe_ and _aroe_ the _frunf_ of the _aroe_ was on _fier_. I shot the _droe_ it went _fluing_ to the cup it lita _flam_. I felt _grate_.

When introducing children to spelling tries, start out by having them fix five words only. For children who have many misspelled words, you might limit corrections to ten words. By working on just a portion of the misspelled words, children are not too discouraged to work through the process. They have a realistic number of words to work with and, therefore, an achievable goal.

The child uses the draft to find the underlined words and attempts to spell this word again in the first column of the Spelling-Tries Sheet. Resources around the room can assist in this process.

SPELLING TRIES			
Name: John			
Date: April 5, 1994			
TRY	TRY AGAIN		CORRECT
flying			
fire			
bo			
aro			
vards			
selver			
franfe			
war			
flam			

Conference 3

1. Work through each word on the child's Spelling-Tries Sheet, offering praise for all spelling attempts made.
2. Rewrite words the child spells correctly in the "Correct" column.
3. If a word still needs fixing, write the letters that are correct, and place dashes in the correct places for the missing letters.
4. Congratulate the child for the parts of the word that are correct.
5. Discuss each word at this time and offer suggestions of how words might be spelled. For example, "The word *bow* does have the *b* and *o* sound. In this word the *o* sound requires two letters, just like in the word *window*."
6. Ask the child to try again.

SPELLING TRIES			
Name: John			
Date: April 5, 1994			
TRY	TRY AGAIN		CORRECT
flying			flying
fire			fire
bo	bo_		
aro	ar_o_		
uards	_ards		
selver	s_lver		
frant	fr_nt		
war	w_r_		
flam	flam_		

Conference 4

1. Congratulate the child again for all attempts made.
2. If a word is spelled correctly, write this word in the "Correct" column.
3. If a word is still incorrect, explain the changes while writing the word in the "Correct" column.

SPELLING TRIES			
Name: John			
Date: April 5, 1994			
TRY	TRY AGAIN		CORRECT
flying			flying
fire			fire
bo	bo w		
aro	ar r o w		
uards	u ards		
selver	s i lver		
frant	fr u nt		
war	w a r e		
flam	flam e		

The child used the teacher's guidelines, word-attack skills, and resources in the room to try spelling the words again.

The child now has a list of all the correctly spelled words to use in publishing. The third column on the Spelling-Tries Sheet is left completely blank. This is done so that the child can more easily read all the correct spellings from the final column without being confused by misspelled words in a nearby column. The spelling try is dated and kept in the child's writing file for evaluation purposes.

SPELLING TRIES			
Name: John			
Date: April 5, 1994			
TRY	TRY AGAIN		CORRECT
flying			flying
fire			fire
bo	bo w		bow
aro	arro w		arrow
uards	u ards		yards
selver	si lver		silver
frante	fru nt		front
war	wa r e		were
flam	flam e		flame

Individual Dictionaries

The child now writes words from the Spelling-Tries Sheet directly into an individual dictionary. These words are now ready for the child to use at any time. By writing words directly into individual dictionaries there is no need for the child to refer to the Spelling-Tries Sheet again.

Publishing

The child rewrites the draft consulting the individual dictionary when coming to a word that is underlined.

STAGE FOUR: WORKING WITH DRAFTS

The child works through the same procedures as discussed in Step three. At the completion of the spelling tries the child writes the correct spelling directly onto the draft above the original spelling attempt. Finally, the child writes the words from the spelling tries in the individual dictionary for future use. The spelling tries are then filed for evaluation purposes.

> Volcanoes can be very dangerous. Most of the volcanoes happen around the tropical areas like Figi [Figi] Africa's rift [rutt] valley the Atlantic Ocean and many other places [plases].

Moving Towards an Individual Spelling Program

The proofreading steps previously described are intended to be guidelines to help you move towards introducing each child to the Individual Spelling Program (see Chapter 7). I use the proofreading steps in the following way:

Children at Stage One: Children at this stage are not involved in the Individual Spelling Program. Instead, they are working through the Individual Writing Program (see Chapter 4). However they are still involved in all other spelling activities in the classroom including passing, group, and whole-class targets (see Chapter 6).

Children at Stage Two: Children at this stage who are beginning to use visual cues while writing and have established some vocabulary are ready for the Individual Spelling Program. The words that these children select come directly from their writing and they only select those words that they already have correct. Using known words at first lets these children concentrate on becoming familiar with the new spelling program. Also, children at this stage may know where to find words for their writing, but may not be able to spell them independently. Giving these children the opportunity to work with words they have written correctly builds confidence.

Children at Stage Three and Four: Children at this point have grasped the basic spelling concepts and are building greater word-attack skills into their repertoire. They are now responsible for learning the correct spelling of previously misspelled words.

The Individual Spelling Program is just one part of the teaching of spelling. For a complete description of how the Individual Spelling Program works, see Chapter 7.

Chapter Six

SPELLING
Selecting
Target Areas

Every time children come in contact with print they have the opportunity to understand more about spelling. You can help ensure that the print is purposeful and varied.

Spelling targets can also help. Spelling targets develop knowledge and awareness of words by focusing children's attention on specific words, blends, and so on, over a period of time, such as a week. In implementing this part of the spelling program, you'll also help children develop the following strategies:

- having a positive attitude to spelling,
- becoming word watchers,
- using visual memory,
- sounding out words—using sound/symbol knowledge,
- using units of meaning—morphemic cues,
- risk taking and inventing spelling,
- comparing relationships between words,
- proofreading skills, and
- using resources to assist with spelling.

I have found that by planning my program around four target areas I can involve children in more meaningful language and spelling activities. At the same time, this structure helps me find a balance between using modeled writing samples, individual writing, and published texts to explore words. The four targets are:

- Passing targets
- Group targets
- Class targets
- Individual targets

PASSING TARGETS

Passing targets encourage children to become word watchers. While involved in reading and writing, children can also be absorbing word structure, patterns, and irregularities found in the language. When reading a big book, sharing children's work, or modeling a particular writing style it is easy to quickly share interesting words with children. This could be a blend of letters such as the *ch* in *cheese* and *choir*. The same blend is there, but a different sound represented. You might highlight the presence of a silent letter in words such as *knee* and *knew*, or a collection of rhyming words: *I*, *eye*, *try*, and *buy*. Whatever the target, the important outcome is that children begin to pay more attention to words and letters, their structure, and their sounds.

By taking advantage of quick interludes with words, children soon become very good detectives and begin to share similar findings with the class. Using passing targets also provides a good model for children who see you thinking and talking about spelling. Children will eagerly copy that positive model.

These passing targets need to be diverse enough to cover the range of understanding suitable for each child. There are often occasions when an incidental discussion about a particular word will be a positive learning outcome for just one student. That's terrific! The sharing of information and the attention given to words and language structure is the key. It's also good to use passing targets to revise and reinforce what children already know.

You and your students can share passing targets during whole-class discussions, group activities, and individual conferences. Once children become used to informal discussions of words, I find that they often share observations without my input. This interest is the key to learning about language through language rather than in isolation. One important rule I like to follow is: "Never tell children what they can tell you."

The other thing I have noticed is that "incidental" learning is extremely valuable. It isn't always necessary to preplan what a passing target will be. This is particularly true when children become the key participants.

However, it's a good idea for you to keep track of passing targets. As these sharing times are brief, activities and further research relative to the target (for example, *ch* words) might not occur immediately after your discussion. By keeping note of the encounter and who shared contributions with the

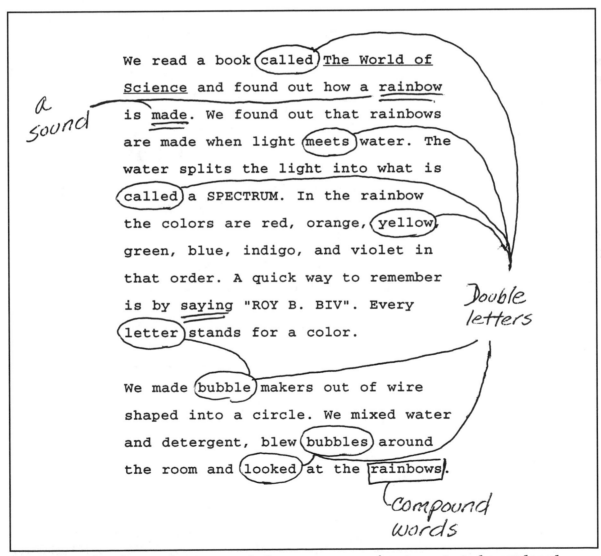

A portion of a class science report shows some passing targets to be explored.

group, you will be able to assist individual children, small groups, or the entire class in future sessions. Using this approach can help you stay on track and avoid drifting away from your original objective for a particular session. It's important to make room for a quick discussion, and then the session continues as planned.

GROUP TARGETS

Sometimes several children require work on a common area. For example, during a writing session, I might find that there are three or four children who are having difficulty dropping the *e* when adding *ing* such as in *baking*, *making*, and *sliding*. Or, I might notice that a few children are uncertain of how to use charts and reference books in the room for spelling.

These needs become group targets, or common spelling problems that a small group of children can focus on together. There are a couple of ways to approach group targets. In the case of *ing*, I would take note of those children needing assistance and plan a separate conference session to address that need during the regular timetable. For example, after looking at the target (*ing*) and completing follow-up activities, we might build a chart together by collecting *ing* words from references around the room. In the second case, I might take time during a writing session to gather children who need help using charts for spelling. With a student's writing sample, I would show how I could use available references. For example, if the word in question is *their*, I might direct children to the chart listing the 100 Most-Used Words. After discussing other suggestions and resources, children continue with their writing.

Group targets are useful because they let you focus your attention on smaller groups of children and monitor their progress more effectively. Group targets also let you avoid going over known and familiar skills with children who don't require the instruction. Once again, it is essential that you keep an account of group targets by recording who was involved, what the target was, what activities children completed, and any follow-up work that may be necessary.

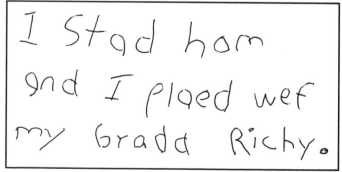

Through their writing, several children have shown a need to talk about the ed *suffix.*

CLASS TARGETS

There will always be occasions when you need to share a new skill or knowledge with the entire class. This is what I call the class target. Class targets are shared with the entire class as part of a preplanned activity during a skills session. After addressing the target, you can involve everyone in a follow-up activity using the acquired skill or knowledge.

If, for example, you identify the initial sound *p* as a class target, you might read the verse "Peter, Peter, Pumpkin Eater" from a chart. The emphasis is on the letter *p*. You might invite children to brainstorm all the words they can think of that start with the letter *p* and go on a *p* hunt, seeking words that have the initial letter *p*. List children's contributions on a chart for all to see.

If you find that some children have difficulty with any of the activities, you might then identify the same skill as a group target and review the skill in a separate session. Finally, it's very important to link the class target with a realistic and appropriate activity. Isolated discussions of blends just for the sake of covering the skill won't be a worthwhile task for children, nor will it be enjoyable for you. Sharing books and student writing samples are two ways to provide follow-up activities. If that's not possible, improvise—look for the target in follow-up writing activities or reinforce a class target from a previous reading or writing session that is still fresh in children's minds.

Homophones are the source of this class target.

INDIVIDUAL TARGETS

Passing, group, and class targets all help children acquire the spelling skills they need. Independence and responsibility are important, too. The individual target is one way of helping your students achieve these skills.

The individual target is a completely individualized spelling program that makes children responsible for learning about words that are important to them. These words might come from writing they've done or are about to do. Children focus on targets they select for one-week periods, following a routine and completing activities that will assist them in learning the words.

Once you have established the individual program in your classroom, you'll find that children enjoy the independence and responsibility. You will also be able to use individual target time for group target activities or other conferences. The following chapter sets out the complete procedure for developing an Individual Spelling Program for your classroom. It's well worth the effort!

Here is an example of how each target area is used over a one-week period.

Week Beginning Nov. 16			
TARGET GROUP	**TARGET AREA**	**SOURCE**	**COMMENT**
PASSING TARGET	*e* sound: *see*, *me*	Brown Bear, Brown Bear, What Do You See?	Grant. Sparkled lots of interest. Follow up with class target.
GROUP TARGET (Sue, Mike, Jo)	*a* sound represented in a number of ways (pl<u>a</u>ed - played)	From individual writing session	Activity: Collect words that have *a* sound (e.g., *ai*, *ay*, *eigh*); group according to letter blend representing the sound.
CLASS TARGET	As above—*a* sound	Share collection made by group target above	Continue above activity as a class resource chart for future use.
INDIVIDUAL TARGET (whole class)	syllables	words selected from individual "zoo report"	Activity: Children write their words, then write again with each syllable in a different color.

Chapter Seven

THE INDIVIDUAL SPELLING PROGRAM

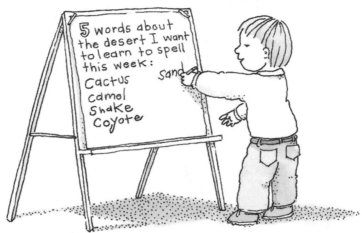

Sharing word-attack and research skills with small groups or an entire class is an excellent way to build up your spelling program. Exposure to word structure, letter combinations, word origin, and letter-sound relationships is all part of developing competent, confident spellers. Children also need practice in being able to recall familiar words and components of words to build new ones. How can you do this with all the words every child is going to need?

The Individual Spelling Program is designed to assist you with giving children opportunities to practice their own words and reinforce word-building skills that meet each child's needs. The program is based on a weekly routine of developing spelling strategies by using words children have selected to learn. Each week they select a different group of words. As each child is responsible for his or her own selection, no two children select exactly the same words.

The exciting thing about the program is the responsibility children take for their own learning. The practical component of this program is that, regardless of the words they choose, students can use all the activities and games. It's also great to have a routine that children are familiar with and enjoy.

How the Individual Target Program Works

Children follow the same five steps each week to learn the words they choose.

1. Children are responsible for selecting words that they would like to learn that week.
2. These selected words are recorded.
3. Children write their words on individual cards and place them in their word banks.
4. During the week, children complete a range of activities or tasks using their words.
5. At the end of the week, children are challenged to see which words they have learned to spell.
6. Children select from a variety of ways to assess their work.

1. WORD SELECTION

The need to spell is a result of the writing process. The words that children select as individual targets each week should be those words that they have been using in their own writing. These words can come from many areas such as journals, projects, stories, and any other curriculum areas where writing has been involved.

There are occasions when you may assist children with word selection. For example, some children may overlook commonly used words that they have misspelled. Although children may be assisted with word selection, the words still come from their writing.

Children may also be guided in choosing words for future use. For example, your class may have brainstormed a range of words for a unit of work currently being studied. If your students know they will need these words at some time during the unit, they may decide to select some of those words as individual targets.

Children may also have an interest in word families or base words they see during group target sessions. They may decide to learn more words within the same framework.

Children who are good spellers or safe spellers can be encouraged to select alternatives for words they are constantly using in their writing.

For example: *said—gasped, exclaimed, announced, screeched*

good—fabulous, fantastic, excellent, superb

The essential element here is that children select their words independently or with your support, and the words chosen are meaningful and have purpose because they have originated from their writing or will be used in future writing sessions. When introducing the program, you might suggest that students select five words. If you feel that students are able to work with more words, try ten.

2. RECORDING WORDS

Individual Dictionaries: As children use correct spellings from the Spelling-Tries, charts, lists, books, and so on, they also place these words into their individual dictionaries (see Chapter 5). If so, the words that they select for individual targets will come directly from their individual dictionaries. Through this strategy, the words students select are already recorded.

If children choose words they plan to use, then they can add these words to their individual dictionaries at the time of selection. Therefore, every word children choose as targets will be found in their individual dictionaries.

Target Books: You might also like to introduce target books. Children use target books to list the words they select on a weekly basis. Children are responsible for writing their own words into the target book and for dating the entries. (You might do this for young children.) As well as being a reference tool, this book gives children an opportunity to write their words for another purpose. Remember, the more often children write their words, the greater the chance they have of learning to spell those words correctly.

Target books enable you to see the words children choose from one week to the next and provide evaluation samples at the same time. By keeping track of the words children select, you can better assist with word selection.

3. WORD-BANK CARDS

Children write each target word on a blank card and place the cards in their individual word banks. (It's a good idea for children to write their initials on the back of each card so that misplaced or dropped cards can be returned to their owners.)

The word banks become the major tool for spelling activities through the week. Rather than pulling out Spelling-Tries Sheets, drafts of writing, dictionaries, or spelling lists, all they need is the word bank. Children will refer to their Word-Bank cards every time they do an individual spelling activity.

Children get a lot of pleasure out of using the word banks and take pride in their personal ownership of them.

The word banks are particularly useful for activities such as:
- grouping words according to a particular criteria—words with common sounds or number of syllables;
- placing words into alphabetical order;
- putting words into order according to the number of letters in each word;
- Look, Say, Cover, Write, Check;
- Word-Bank Bingo (p. 90);
- Sunk (p. 86); and
- Spell of the Century (p. 89).

While children are writing out their Word-Bank cards, you can rove around asking individual children to read their words to you. At the same time you can check to ensure that the words are written correctly.

It is important to point out that each week children will select new words and make new Word-Bank cards. Have children remove the old Word-Bank cards at the end of each week.

4. ACTIVITIES

During the week, the children will complete a range of activities designed to assist them in learning their weekly words and developing a greater understanding of word structure. Chapter 8 describes a selection of activities you can use. You might also look for activities in other publications and adapt other games and activities for your spelling program.

5. WEEKLY CHALLENGE

At the end of each week, children are challenged to see how well they learned their words. It is important that children have a procedure to follow so that each week's challenge is a positive learning experience. During this time it is important that the classroom is extremely quiet. You might give this session a special name such as DEAR time (Drop Everything And Read), so that the children do remember to work quietly. I call it "Respect Time."

This booklet becomes another valuable evaluation piece for the child and the teacher.

The term *challenge* is used as opposed to the word *test* since this entire program focuses on individual children and their ongoing responsibilities. Children are responsible for their own results and are not compared with others. The materials required each week for the challenges are Individual Word Banks, Individual-Target Challenge booklets, and a pencil.

There are a number of ways to present the weekly challenge:

Individual Challenges: Children challenge themselves by using the "Look, Say, Cover, Write, Check" procedure.

1. Collect your Target Challenge booklet, Word Bank, and pencil.
2. Write the date on your new Challenge page.
3. Take your Word-Bank cards out of your Word Bank.
4. Place them upside down on the table.
5. Take one Word-Bank card.
6. Look at the word.
7. Say the word to yourself.
8. Cover the word.
9. Write the word.
10 Check the word.
11. If the word is correct, give it a checkmark.
12. If the word needs fixing, underline the tricky part.
13. Put this card back into your word bank.
14. Repeat steps 5 to 13 with the rest of your words.

Peer Challenges: The peer challenge gives children the opportunity to work with a partner during challenge time.

1. Collect materials—Word-Bank cards, Target Challenge booklet, pencil.
2. Write the date on a new Target Challenge page.
3. Exchange Word-Bank cards with your partner and place them upside down on the table.
4. Take a card and hold it up for your partner to see.
5. Ask your partner to look at the word and read it aloud.
6. Cover the word.
7. Have your partner write the word.
8. Repeat steps 4–7 with the remaining words.

9. Check through the words with your partner using the correct model as a guide.
10. Place a checkmark next to words that are correct. Underline the tricky part of words that are incorrect.
11. Switch roles and carry out the same procedure, from step 4–10.

A peer challenge.

Group Challenges: The same steps apply as with the peer challenge except that you show the word to each individual and then read it. You may also put the word into a sentence. If children sit in a circle, a simple clockwise rotation occurs.

A group challenge.

You show word one to the first child then move to child two and show his or her first word, and so on. This continues around the circle so that while you show a word to one child the rest of the children are writing their own words or waiting for their next turn.

Once the routine is established, the group challenges usually take only about 25 minutes to complete for an entire class. In a group challenge, children are still responsible for checking their words and underlining the tricky parts on those words that need fixing. You might correct the challenges for young children as they sit alongside.

While group challenges are underway, the remainder of the class might be:

- practicing their words ready for their challenge,
- doing quiet reading,
- doing quiet writing, or
- completing any other assigned tasks.

The main consideration during this time is a quiet working atmosphere.

Note: Group challenges and peer challenges can be completed with cross-age groups. The weekly challenge is also a good time to invite parents in to help.

6. WEEKLY ASSESSMENT

Individual Dictionaries: After a challenge, children take out their individual dictionaries and place a checkmark beside the words that they spelled correctly. This helps children keep a record of the words they have attempted and spelled; so that in weeks to come, they don't keep selecting the same words.

The words that students still have trouble with are left without a checkmark. In following weeks students can select those words again if they choose. In keeping with the focus on responsibility, it is essential that this decision is left up to the children.

Word-Bank Cards: Children can throw away cards featuring words they still had trouble with. There is no need to keep them at all. If the child ever needs to use those words again, they can be found in the individual dictionary. If the child would like to give the words another try, then they just become part of a new week's selection. The most important thing is that each week children get a fresh start with individual targets.

Cards featuring the words the children spelled correctly can be used in a number of ways, including:

Word Savers: Cards featuring the words that children got correct can now be placed in their Word-Saver containers. This builds up from week to week so that by the end of the year children have a large selection of words they have learned. Word-Saver cards can be used throughout the year for sorting and classifying words, putting words into a particular order, writing imaginative stories using a number of chosen words, playing Word-Bank bingo, and many other activities.

Target Collection: Each child can keep a scrap book marking each page with a letter of the alphabet. This book becomes a Target Collection book. At the end of a challenge, the cards featuring words a child spells correctly can be pasted into the Target Collection book.

This book now features all the words the child has success with. Children love to go back and reread all of these words. By using a Target Collection book, children have a concrete reminder of their weekly achievements.

Word Saver/Target Collection Combination: The above suggestions may be combined so that each card is collected in a Word Saver to be used for activities throughout the year. At the end of the year, children put their words into alphabetical order and then paste them in their Target Collection books.

Plan on a period of time each day for two or three weeks to complete this task. At the end, children each have a book to take home and be very proud of.

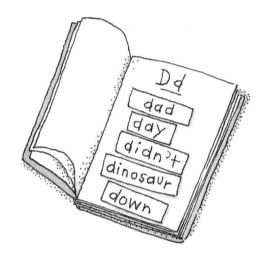

Class Charts: Bulletin boards related to a current unit of work can serve as a base for displaying related words that children spell correctly. At the end of a challenge children add their Word-Bank cards to the display. The display resembles a collage of words and is a great resource for children to use when searching for words. Children enjoy helping others find words on the board, especially when the words are theirs.

Some of the displays my students and I have enjoyed creating include:

- a hot air balloon (with the words filling the balloon),
- a volcano (with words erupting out of the volcano—I used red, black, and grey colored paper for Word-Bank cards),
- gingerbread house (with words coating the house),
- a magic carpet (I used four colors for Word-Bank cards so that I could create a patchwork design), and
- a rocket ship (we just used grey Word-Bank cards for this).

Other Word-Bank card activities include:

- predicting how long it will take the class to learn a room full of words. Children join their words to make a long chain and continue the chain around the room until they return to the start. This incorporates lots of math too.
- putting Word-Bank cards into a Big Mystery box. Draw a mystery word each day and invite the entire class to learn to spell it together, as well as discover something special about that word. This may lead to looking at letter combinations and the sounds they make. The owner of the word becomes the Word Wizard for the day.

- making a giant card, pasting learned Word-Bank cards inside, and presenting it to parents.
- adding Word-Bank cards together for a class total and graphing to observe progress over a period of time.
- making individual graphs by pasting individual Word-Bank cards onto separate graphs and collecting results for a period of time.

Week 2 and Beyond

At the beginning of each new week children have empty word banks and are ready to select their new target words. The routine is repeated.

Chapter Eight

SPELLING ACTIVITIES

To keep your spelling program exciting for both yourself and your student, you'll need to continue introducing as many stimulating and varied spelling activities as possible. This will help to give the regular weekly routine a novel appeal. Your own teaching style and the amount of responsibility you like to give your students will determine the way you introduce and use spelling activities.

As with any new program, it's important that you feel comfortable with the implementation and organization of the contents. Keep in mind that the more responsibility you allow your students, the more opportunities you'll have to include conferences and group targets in your regular timetable.

Following are several ways you might organize spelling activities in your classroom.

ORGANIZING YOUR SPELLING ACTIVITIES

Weekly Contract: Create a contract that outlines a number of activities children can complete during the week. An individual contract might look like this:

CRAIG'S CONTRACT
1. Look for the same first letter.
2. Find small words in big words.

CLASS CONTRACT
1. Make your words using letters from newspaper headlines.
2. Find two words with the same final sound.

Spelling Sessions: Set aside a number of sessions during the week for completing a nominated activity each time.

Round Robin Spelling Session: Divide the class into groups. Each group completes a different activity during each session, then rotate until all activities are completed by the entire class. For example:

Day: Monday		
GROUP A	**GROUP B**	**GROUP C**
Word Values	Penman Sentences	Sunk
Penman Sentences	Sunk	Word Values
Sunk	Word Values	Penman Sentences

Conferences: In the Round Robin, incorporate a time to conduct spelling conferences by replacing one of the activities with conference time.

Choice Activity: Children contract to complete one specific activity each week. They are then free to complete as many others as they desire.

Language Sessions: Try incorporating individual spelling activities with other language activities.

    Activity 1: Individual Spelling
    Activity 2: Silent Reading
    Activity 3: Literature Writing
    Activity 4: Spelling/Writing Conference

Use the Round Robin timetable described above to move students through the various activities.

Once you decide on an organizational strategy that suits your style, you're ready to enjoy sharing any of the activities that follow:

ACTIVITIES FOR INDIVIDUAL TARGET WORDS

Penman Sentences

Children write sentences that include their chosen words. They can underline the week's words or write them in different colors.

Sarah
A caterpillar changes into a <u>butterfly</u>.
On <u>Sunday</u> I went to visit my uncle.
Blue and <u>yellow</u> paint makes green paint.

Children can vary the activity by creating two columns on their papers, writing the words in the first column and their sentences in the other column. This gives children the opportunity to write their words twice during this activity.

Sarah	
butterfly	A caterpillar changes into a <u>butterfly</u>.
Sunday	On <u>Sunday</u> I went to visit my uncle.
yellow	Blue and <u>yellow</u> paint makes green paint.

Children may also cover up the list of words with an index card and Look, Say, Cover, Write, and Check their words on a separate sheet of paper after writing their sentences.

Secret Codes

Children use an alphabet code to write their words in secret.

Sample Code:

a = 1	f = 6	k = 11	p = 16	u = 21	z = 26
b = 2	g = 7	l = 12	q = 17	v = 22	
c = 3	h = 8	m = 13	r = 18	w = 23	
d = 4	i = 9	n = 14	s = 19	x = 24	
e = 5	j = 10	o = 15	t = 20	y = 25	

Children first write their words correctly. Then they rewrite their words in secret code.

Simon	
went	**23, 5, 14, 20**
riding	**18, 9, 4, 9, 14, 7**
friend	**6, 18, 9, 5, 14, 4**

Children can now cover up their words and decode the secret spellings to reveal their words. They can check their decoded words with the words in their list.

Children will also enjoy creating their own secret codes using symbols in place of numbers.

Word Values

Children write down their first word, calculate the value of their word by using the code above, and repeat the process with their remaining words.

a	= 1+1	f	= 5+2	k	= 2+7	p	= 5+4	u	= 7+4	z	= 4+0
b	= 2+1	g	= 9+1	l	= 5+5	q	= 2+8	v	= 6+0		
c	= 3+2	h	= 7+3	m	= 6+3	r	= 3+3	w	= 5+0		
d	= 4+4	i	= 6+2	n	= 7+1	s	= 4+5	x	= 3+1		
e	= 2+3	j	= 4+3	o	= 2+2	t	= 2+6	y	= 5+3		

You can change the codes to support other mathematical skills. Children can also substitute the secret code values above.

Andrew	
party	p = 9 a = 2 r = 6 t = 8 y = 8 party = 33

Word Finds

Children have fun creating their own word finds by first listing their words on a piece of paper and then placing each word into a grid. They will enjoy going back to their word finds the following day to find their words all over again. Children can Look, Say, Cover, Find, and Check their words.*(Note the substitution of the word* Find *for* Write.*)*

w	**e**	**n**	**t**	g		went
i	y	h	o	b		out
t	h	**o**	**u**	t		with
h	h	m	s	**o**		too
a	f	r	g	**o**		

Giving children an attractive grid adds to the fun.

Rainbow Words

Children write their words in list form and then write over the word two (or more) times using different colors to create rainbow words.

Book Titles

Children select one of their words, and write a title for a new book that includes the word.

My word	Book title
for	A Gift for Mary

Children might like to illustrate book jackets for their titles. Use the book jackets as springboards to other activities.

- Display book jackets and let children use them as story starters.
- Invite children to make oral predictions about what they will find when they open each book.
- Have small groups write cooperative stories using one of the book titles. Share the stories and notice how different each group's story is from the others.

Ransom Words

Children write their words in list form. They now cut out letters from newspapers or magazines to make their words. Children can paste their newspaper-print words beside their written words.

	Michelle
beach	B e a c H
out	o U t
from	f R o M

Word Frames

Children write their words. They write each word again, drawing a frame around each to show the body, tail, and head of each letter.

Choice

Children write their words in list form, then complete a Choice activity with their words. You might select several Choice activities for children's weekly contracts. Choice activities are also good for early finishers. Plan on one choice per session. Sample choice activities include:

- Write the vowels in one color and the consonants in another.
- Underline a letter pattern and write another word with the same pattern.
- Write a word that rhymes with your word.
- Write all the smaller words that are in your word (hidden words).
- Underline the tricky part in your word.
- Write another word that has the same first letter.
- Underline a sound and write another word with the same sound in it.
- Write an alternative word.
- Find your word in the dictionary and write the word that comes after it.
- Change your word by adding a prefix or a suffix, or making it plural.
- Make word frames.
- Use the Look, Say, Cover, Write, Check method.

My words	Hidden words
party	pa
shopping	shop, hop, pin, in
yesterday	yes, day

My words	Hidden words	1st letter words	Rhyming words
face	ace	fish, fast, fat, fun	race, chase
too	to	tap, top, tin	shoe, blue, moo

Word Search

Children pick something special about each of their words, for example: initial letters, letter blends such as *ch ie*, or interesting endings such as *ed*, *ing*, and *es*. They now find and record as many words as they can with the same characteristic. When doing this activity, recommend that children focus on one word and one characteristic per session.

Sunk

Children work in pairs. One child selects a word from a partner's Word Bank and writes a dash to represent each letter. The other child has to spell the word correctly by guessing letters. When the child gets a letter correct it is written in the correct location. If a letter is incorrect the boat begins to sink. Both children double check the word at the end of the game. Children take turns, sharing one word at a time.

Step-Ups

The child places Word-Bank cards face up on the table, selects one word as the starting word, and writes it down. The word card then goes back in the Word Bank. Next, the child uses the last letter of the starting word as the first letter of a new word. If there's not a word in the Word Bank that works, the child can choose one from around the room. The last letter of this word then becomes the first letter of the next word. This continues until the child has used up all of the Word-Bank words. Children can record the number of steps they make and try to beat their own scores the next time they play.

This is also an ideal activity for cooperative groups.

Crosswords

Children can create their own crosswords with their words. To begin, they can just list their words (rather than write clues) and then design the crossword. This is a fun activity to share with classmates.

Letters and Words

Children place their Word-Bank words in front of them and then use alphabet cards to reconstruct their words. This is a good activity for using the Look, Say, Cover, Make, Check activity. *(Note the substitution of the word* Make *for* Write.*)*

Take Cover

This game is played in pairs. Players place their Word-Bank cards face up in front of them. Player one looks carefully at his or her words and then looks away. Player two removes one card. Player one looks again and then writes down the missing word. Both players check the spelling of the written word. Players continue the game, taking turns.

Change One

The child writes one word down and then creates new words by changing one letter from the original word. This continues until the child has created ten new words.

fish – fist – fast – last – lost – most – mist – mint – hint – hind

Displays

Sometimes it's fun to combine word activities with another kind of activity such as paper folding, paper tearing, or paper scrunching. For example, during spring children can cut out flowers, write their words in the petals, fill the center with scrunched up paper, and display their blooms in bunches around the room. Below are ideas you might want to use.

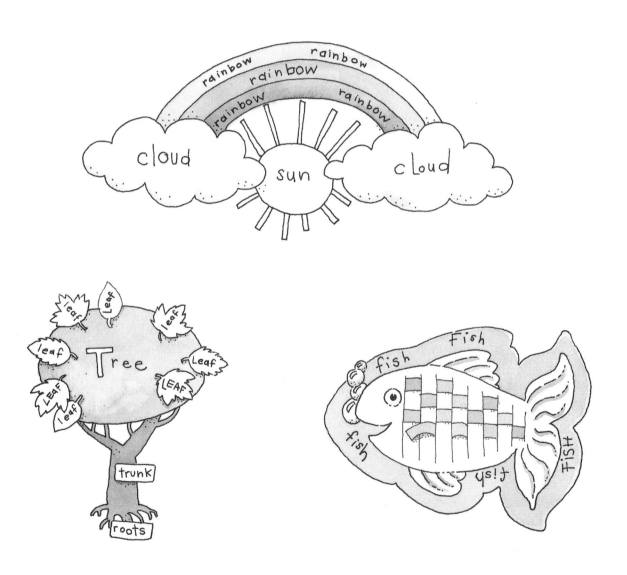

ACTIVITIES FOR THE CLASS AND SMALL GROUPS

Here are some activities that are lots of fun for the whole class or for small groups. You can use them as quick, attention-getting introductions for language sessions, as springboards to spelling investigations, or to add to your classroom resources. They'll encourage word-watching and word-thinking and promote enthusiasm for spelling in your classroom.

Spell of the Century

Three children are selected as contestants. Each contestant has a mini blackboard and chalk. You (or a student) call out a word and the contestants must write down the word and turn the board around for all to see. The first child to show the correct spelling gets one point. The winner is the first child with 5 points.

Spell of the Century words can be collected during the year from units studied, commonly misspelled words, interesting words, and so on.

An alternative is to have children take turns calling out words from their Word Banks.

Troop Words

Children work in small groups for this activity. The class decides on two categories of interest, such as *names* and *foods* or *places* and *animals*. Each group writes the name of each category on a piece of paper that is divided or folded into columns. Play begins when you call out a letter of the alphabet. This letter becomes the initial letter players use to create a word in each category. Group members work together to fill in each column. The first group to finish calls out "troop words." The winning group shares their words. One point is scored for an "original" word, while zero is scored for a word that more than one group uses.

letter	a name	a food
W	Wendy	watermelon
C	Claire	candy
B	Bill	bread

Categories

Children work in small groups for this activity. Each group has a sheet of paper divided into three columns. You announce a word characteristic such as double letters, *ing* or *sh* words, first letter *t*, or three syllables. Each group writes as many words as possible featuring this characteristic in a set time limit. When time's up, each group shares its findings. Repeat the procedure two or more times.

Children can get to know classroom aids such as picture books, factual texts, and charts around the room with this activity, using the materials to find words with the feature characteristic. It's also a great way to generate words for class charts and class targets.

Categories Relay

This is similar to the previous activity. Children are divided into groups and each group has a sheet of paper divided into three columns and headed with similar items as in the Categories game. Place each group's paper at the front of the room. When you call "Go," the first member of each team fills in a word in any column and rushes back to tag the next team member. The second team member fills in another word in any column and tags the next team member. This continues until the teacher calls "Stop." Groups add up their words—the group with the most words wins.

Word-Bank Bingo

Children place all of their Word-Bank cards face up on the table. You call out clues from a set of Word-Bank Bingo cards. When children find a word that matches the clue, they return this word to their Word Banks. The first child to return all words to the bank calls out "Word-Bank Bingo."

Sample clues:

- a word beginning with *s*
- a word with 5 letters
- a word that has 4 consonants
- a word that ends in *ed*
- a word with *th*

You might want to keep extra sets of Word-Bingo cards handy so that small groups or pairs of children can play on their own.

When introducing the game, it helps to focus on one criteria, for example "a word beginning with ____ ." You might then introduce "a word with ____ letters ." As you introduce more skills and word knowledge in your spelling program you can add them to your Word-Bank Bingo clues.

Story Chains

Divide the class into small groups and give each group a piece of paper on which you've written a story starter. Children take turns adding one word at a time to tell a story. Groups can share their stories with the class. Children can also work together to make necessary changes and proofread the text for spelling errors.

Letter Lotto

Select 12 alphabet cards at random. Have children work in groups to create as many words as they can by using those letters.

Catch Words

Give small groups of children a collection of blank mini-cards. Each group searches the room for words with a particular characteristic that you (or a student) suggests, such as compound words, words with double letters in them, initial letters, or words with two syllables. Children write the words they find on the mini-cards, check each other's words, and place the cards in the group collection. Each group tries to find as many words as it can.

You can use these mini-cards to create a class chart, word tin, or word book for children to use while writing.

Alphabet Relay

Give pairs or small groups of children a collection of ten words or letters to work with. After placing the cards face down, students try to put the words into alphabetical order as follows:

- When you say "Go," the first player turns over one card and tags the next player.
- Player 2 turns over the next card and places it where it belongs.
- The relay continues until all the cards are turned over.
- The team checks the order and makes any changes.
- The first team to call "Alpha" has its collection checked. If all ten cards are in order, then the team wins.

Board Games

To play this game you'll need dice, a playing piece for each player, players' Word Banks, and a simple board game that includes an easy path with instructions written on some steps of the path, for example:

- go back one space
- have another turn
- miss a turn
- move forward one space
- challenge

Players take turns throwing the dice and moving around the board. When landing on a challenge, the player must spell a Word-Bank word. The first person to reach the finish line, wins.

Trick Words

Children play this game in groups or pairs. To begin, write part of a word on the board with dashes for each missing letter. Each team has one minute to list as many words as possible that could be the trick word.

| _ _ _ t |
| _ e a _ |

beat, sort, foot, mart, chat, meat, meet, seat, sift team, beam, heat, meat, meal, dear, tear, bean

Pick a Tin

Label two tins—*Spell* and the other *Tell*. Place a series of mini-cards with special clues written on them in each tin. Each Spell card has one word written on it. Each Tell card has a clue on it similar to those from Word Bingo (for example, words that start with *bl*). Select a player to pick a *Spell* or *Tell* card. Children choosing *Spell* cards must spell the words correctly. For *Tell* cards children say words that fit the clue. Each player has three turns before choosing another player.

Blenders

Decide on a letter blend or combination, such as *sh*. Ask each child to list letters that combine with the blend to make words. For example, a student might list *ed*, *oe*, *op*, *wi*, *eet*, *fiing*. Students swap papers with partners and try to figure out the whole words (*shed*, *shoe*, *shop*, *wish*, *sheet*, *fishing*). Children now share their whole words. You may find this a good opportunity for developing class targets or creating new resources such as topic tins, word charts, or word books.

Chapter Nine

RECORD KEEPING AND EVALUATION

Ongoing and practical evaluation is a key component in all successful classroom programs. Individual children's performances, your own performance, and program effectiveness are all part of the evaluation process. Together, these three components provide information for future program planning, as well as for forming short and long-term objectives.

When evaluating spelling, it's helpful to remember its connection to the entire writing process. Spelling evaluation can provide a general overview of your writing program. If you find that children are not using a variety of writing styles, then you might need to rethink your integrated units. In planning future units, you can be sure to include opportunities for more variation.

Evaluation strategies may vary—from reviewing students' work to conducting conferences and creating checklists. Keep in mind, though, that time-consuming evaluation forms and an overabundance of documentation can detract from valuable teaching and planning time. Therefore an effective evaluation system should be well prepared and time efficient.

This chapter suggests ways you can use three of the most valuable resources for spelling evaluation:

- children's work,
- your records, and
- your program plans.

EVALUATING USING CHILDREN'S WORK

To become proficient spellers, children work through several distinguishable developmental stages. There are times when one piece of writing may reflect more than one spelling stage. When looking at spelling performance it is necessary to observe the skills required to become a proficient speller, rather than merely addressing words that children know.

A convenient way to assist with spelling evaluation is to look at the three groups that describe spelling development within the context of writing:

1. Beginning/Reluctant Writers

At this stage children are putting pen to paper. They understand that written symbols convey messages and that each symbol or group of symbols represents a particular sound. Children are beginning to understand writing conventions such as directionality. These children are encouraged to use phonetic concepts and invented spelling in their writing.

2. Developing Writers

Children at this level are developing a greater understanding of the structure of words. They rely less heavily on letter-sound relationships and begin to use visual cues while writing. They are also developing the knowledge that sounds can be represented by different letters and that letters can represent more than one sound.

3. Established Writers

Children at this level have grasped basic spelling concepts, are increasing their understanding of word structure, and are building greater word-attack skills into their writing repertoire.

As well as considering the three groups, effective spelling evaluation looks at students' attitudes and confidence when attempting unknown words, the way they use references to support spelling, and their proofreading skills. Dating work samples and ensuring children's work is stored appropriately will facilitate the evaluation process.

Beginning Writers' Program: The four-grid system described in Chapter 4 provides a week-by-week sample of work completed by the child. This book serves as an ideal evaluation tool as it is easy to refer back one week at a time to see the stages of development taking place.

Personal Writing: Children's diaries are also a good source of information, particularly if they are written in on a regular basis.

Writing Files: Dated samples of children's work kept in their writing files can also assist with evaluation. The two folders in each file, as described in Chapter 2, put students' ongoing and previous work at your fingertips. By following a routine from the start of the year, children are able to look after their own writing files appropriately. You can refer to work in both folders to evaluate proofreading strategies and writing styles attempted.

Spelling Tries: Dated copies of spelling tries should be kept in children's folders. By using the design presented in this book (see Chapter 5), where the final column is kept intact, you can always determine intended spelling.

Individual Dictionaries: Flipping through students' individual dictionaries helps in a number of ways. The number of words listed, the number check-marked, and the type of words students list all give information about spelling strategies students are using.

Weekly Challenges and Words for the Week: Browsing through these two booklets reveals the types of words children are attempting to learn and those that they have learned. It also reveals problem areas where children have underlined tricky parts of words misspelled.

EVALUATING USING YOUR RECORDS

There are many strategies available to assist you with documenting your program and student progress. Making good use of children's work samples can help you cut down on the amount of documentation you need to gather. By adding anecdotal information gathered over a period of time, you'll get a well-rounded picture of each student's achievements and areas of need. Here are some ways to manage the process.

Anecdotal Notes: It is useful to have a notebook and pencil on hand at all times to jot down incidental observations. Later, you can transfer this information into each child's individual file.

Student Files: Set up a file for each child that includes a collection of work samples and reports from previous years, current anecdotal notes, profiles, or any other valuable evaluation materials.

Conference Notes: Keep comments and information gathered from individual conferences in each child's individual file.

Checklists and Profiles: Checklists and profiles may be a compulsory component within your school. If so, continue to fill these out on a regular basis. Keep in mind of course, that the information required can also be gathered using any of the strategies described above.

CONFERENCE NOTES
NAME: **John**
DATE: **10/3/93**
COMMENTS: **Unit writing, (party invitation) used thesaurus to find an alternative word for fun.**
DATE: **10/15/93**
COMMENTS: **Unit writing, (party invitation) spelling tries being used**

EVALUATING USING YOUR PROGRAM PLANS

The following suggestions include ways to organize long-term and immediate program ideas. You'll find some that relate to the general integrated program and others that are more specific.

Yearly Planner: An overall picture of units you want to cover through the year is useful for determining just how much variety your program offers. You might find it useful to sketch out specific writing ideas for each unit.

Weekly Planner: The weekly work planner outlines all activities planned for the entire curriculum on a week-by-week basis. It's useful to include a section for daily anecdotal notes.

Writing Areas: Every week the activities planned for each writing area can be recorded. You can use this to note children in need of writing conferences. (For a sample sheet, see page 109.)

	FREE	UNIT	LITERATURE	PERSONAL
WRITING AREAS				
WK	**WRITING**	**WRITING**	**WRITING**	**WRITING**
1	model: card making	wall story of excursion to zoo	rewrite ending "Hungry Giant"	Model: family word book
2	share graffiti board	model: letter writing	predict story content	Model: final sounds
3	suggest continuing with unit writing	draft thank-you letters to vet	insert text into cartoon strip	Model: expanding on ideas

Spelling Targets: Each week, record the activities planned for individual and other spelling targets. (These targets may already be included in your writing activity plans.) In particular, record passing targets shared by children after a group or class activity. (For a sample sheet, see page 110.)

SPELLING TARGETS				
WK	**CLASS**	**PASSING**	**GROUP**	**INDIVIDUAL**
1	ee words from science report	Paula shared ea in team as having same sound as ee	Kate, Tom, Kim: revise tenses	penman sentences, word finds, syllables

Activities Checklist: I find it useful to have a checklist of all the great activities and teaching styles that I would like to share with children during the year. As I browse through new teacher reference materials or learn about new strategies from colleagues, I add the ideas to the checklist. Throughout the year it's useful to refer back to the checklist for new strategies or activities. This helps to ensure children are given lots of variety.

ACTIVITIES	SOURCE
using an overhead projector	
invite a guest speaker	√ Pet care
make jigsaws of children's names	
close exercise	√ Brown Bear, Brown Bear
letter predictions for making new words	
hidden words	
wall story	√ Excursion Follow Up
story map	
cooperative writing task	

Chapter Ten

QUESTIONS AND ANSWERS

Whether you're adapting an existing program or implementing something new, common concerns are bound to arise. Here are the answers to some questions teachers frequently ask.

1. What do you do with children who say they can't write?

One golden rule to share with children is "There's no such thing as *can't*." These children need to be given the confidence to try. This is best achieved in a positive learning environment where constant, positive feedback supports every attempt children make.

Encouraging reluctant writers to illustrate first, then talk about their drawings is also helpful. You might try scribing their ideas, then inviting students to trace over your writing. Chapter 4 outlines a writing program for beginning and reluctant writers and offers a detailed approach to introducing writing to children through their own thoughts. It's a great place to start.

Finally, if you're still having difficulty, try using puppets. I've found that hand puppets work wonders with children. They converse with imaginary characters and even share fears about writing—without being concerned that you're in earshot. You'll be surprised and excited by the results. Give it a try!

2. What do you do with a child who writes pages and pages with very few words spelled correctly?

The most important factor here is that the child wants to write and has the confidence to make approximations while writing. This needs to be encouraged. When it comes to proofreading this work for spelling errors this child should be responsible for only a small portion of the text, such as the beginning or a favorite part.

If spelling tries are used, the child should be responsible for an agreed number of words, say five or ten. This way he or she is still enthusiastic about writing and is still responsible for proofreading and improving spelling strategies.

3. If an entire class is working on the Individual Writing Program, how do you find time to conference each child?

Planning is the key to any successful program. There are a number of ways this can be tackled. Firstly, the children can be responsible for writing in their individual books at different times throughout the day. While the teacher is conferencing, the other children can be working on independent activities such as silent reading, free writing or contracts.

Another alternative is to plan the week so that every day is the first day of the program for a small group of children. In other words, every day a different group of children have a conference while the rest of the group is completing the other weekly activities. Finally, it's great to get parents into the classroom to assist with the writing program. An information session at the start of the year will ensure that parents know exactly what is required of them during an individual conference.

4. I have to use spelling lists as part of the school program. Can I still use some of the strategies in this book?

Certainly. The best types of words for children to learn are those that they require in their writing, but if you are using lists you can still use all four spelling targets in this book. Just because a list is referred to doesn't mean they are the only words children require, nor does it mean they are developing appropriate word-attack skills.

Use the list as a part of the Individual Spelling Program outlined in Chapter 7. Rotate the program on a two-week cycle where one week the children are learning words from the required list and the second week they are learning words from their own writing.

5. What do you do with children who never seem to misspell words in their writing?

First, you need to look at the types of words the children are using. These children may lack confidence and therefore only use known words. Continue to reinforce different spelling strategies, such as using spelling resources during shared discussions and modeled writing sessions.

Secondly, during proofreading sessions, encourage these children to replace overused words. This is a good opportunity to introduce a thesaurus to the children.

6. How do you introduce spelling tries to all areas of the curriculum?

Introducing a new strategy to children takes time and patience. Children can't be expected to grasp an idea immediately.

Introduce the spelling tries to small groups of children during a planned writing session. Work through each step with them until they understand the process involved.

Repeat this procedure a few times, until the children know exactly how the spelling tries work. Then when the children are writing during integrated units, they know how to use spelling tries, and the procedure will become part of everyday writing.

7. Even though parents are happy with their children's progress, I still have some who are concerned with what's actually happening in the writing program. How can I give parents the same confidence I have about my writing program?

One important consideration when it comes to parents, is that unless they have professional backgrounds in education, many of them draw upon their own school experiences to make judgments about their children's schooling.

You can help by making an effort to give parents all the information and feedback they require to understand and have confidence in what their children are experiencing at school. Parent information meetings at the beginning of the school year are a superb way to start this communication. If your school is not already involved in such events, talk to your school administrator and arrange a parent information evening. This is a great time to share your philosophy and to give parents an opportunity to express their concerns.

Throughout the year, follow up your session with newsletters to parents. Inform them about what their children are focusing on and share their successes. Note upcoming events and future instructional focuses. Parents will appreciate your efforts to keep them informed.

8. I have many parents who want to help their children at home with writing. This is great, but I am concerned about their approaches. How can I support parents' efforts and make sure they are using sound strategies?

Parents who are enthusiastic about helping their children will be more than willing to learn what they can do to give additional support. As previously mentioned, parent information evenings are an excellent way to get your parents involved in your classroom approach to writing and other curriculum areas.

Consider having a special meeting with interested parents to address specific areas, such as writing. This will give you an opportunity to explain the importance of different strategies, such as spelling tries. Other ideas to try include:

- share samples of children's writing;

- consider videotaping a writing conference so parents can see the strategies in action; and
- offer a simple checklist of important points that parents can refer to at home.

9. Some parents still want to see spelling lists. How can I use the strategies in this book and satisfy parents' needs, too?

The strategies in this book can support a variety of teaching styles, and can be adapted to suit the needs of your parents, too. When introducing individual targets for spelling (see page 61), encourage children to write their words out in list form to take home and share with parents. The first time you do this, include a note to parents that explains where the words came from and how children are using them in class. Suggest a few activities so that parents can practice the words with their children.

Every now and then, send home another letter explaining different spelling strategies and suggesting activities for learning new words and developing spelling skills.

10. I believe that invented spelling is an important part of a successful writing program. How do the strategies in this book relate to this approach?

While children are writing, they need to be encouraged to make approximations, so that the flow of writing is not interrupted. At the same time, children need to be thinking about what they wish to convey in print and the resources available to help them do so. In other words, giving children a number of strategies, including invented spelling, will help them develop skill and confidence in writing and spelling.

REPRODUCIBLE
SHEETS

SPELLING TRIES

Name:

Date:

TRY	TRY AGAIN		CORRECT

_____'S

WORDS FOR THIS WEEK

Date:

1.

2.

3.

4.

5.

6.

7.

8.

9.

10.

_____'S

CHALLENGE

Date:
1.
2.
3.
4.
5.
6.
7.
8.
9.
10.

WRITING AREA				
WK	FREE WRITING	UNIT WRITING	LITERATURE WRITING	PERSONAL WRITING

INDIVIDUAL SPELLING TARGETS

WEEK	ACTIVITY

THE 100 MOST FREQUENTLY USED WORDS

a	did	her	over	this
about	do	him	people	three
after	dog	his	play	time
all	down	home	ran	to
an	for	just	said	too
and	from	like	saw	two
are	get	little	school	up
as	go	man	see	us
at	going	me	she	very
back	good	morning	so	was
be	got	mother	some	water
because	I	my	soon	we
big	if	night	started	went
but	in	not	that	were
by	into	of	the	what
call	is	off	their	when
came	it	on	them	will
can	had	one	then	with
could	have	our	there	would
day	he	out	they	you

PROFESSIONAL BIBLIOGRAPHY

Bolton F. and Snowball D. *Ideas For Spelling.* Thomas Nelson. Australia, 1985.

Coles M. *Bright Ideas: Word Games.* Scholastic. New York, 1989.

Gentry, R. "An Analysis Developmental Spelling" in GNYS AT WRK. *The Reading Teacher.* Vol. 36, No. 2. November 1982, pp. 192-199.

Jackson N. and Pillow P. *The Reading Writing Workshop: Getting Started.* Scholastic. New York, 1992.

Lacey C. *Creative Connections: Spelling the Fun Way.* Rowe Publications. Australia, 1991.

Parry J. and Hornsby D. *Write On: A Conference Approach to Writing.* Nelson. Australia, 1989.

Powell D. and Hornsby D. *Learning Phonics and Spelling in a Whole Language Classroom.* Scholastic. New York, 1993.

Rowe G. and Lomas B. *Spelling for Writing.* Oxford University Press. New York, 1985.

Schlosser K. and Phillips V. *Beginning in Whole Language.* Scholastic. New York, 1991.